HIV PREVENTION AND CARE

Teaching Modules for Nurses and Midwives

INTERNATIONAL ENCYCLOPAEDIA OF AIDS - 8

HIV PREVENTION AND CARE

Teaching Modules for Nurses and Midwives

Editor

Dr. Digumarti Bhaskara Rao

M.Sc., M.A., M.A., M.Ed., Ph.D.

Reader & Research Director

R.V.R. College of Education

Srinivasa Nagar Colony

Guntur–522 006

(India)

DISCOVERY PUBLISHING HOUSE PVT. LTD.

NEW DELHI-110 002

First Published - 2000

Reprinted - 2017

ISBN: 978-81-7141-465-9 (Set)

ISBN: 978-81-7141-530-4

© Editor

HIV Prevention and Care
Teaching Modules for Nurses and Midwives

Published by:

DISCOVERY PUBLISHING HOUSE PVT. LTD.
4383/4B, Ansari Road Darya Ganj
New Delhi - 110 002 (India)
Phone: +91-11-23279245, 43596064-65
Fax: +91-11-23253475
E-mail: discoverypublishinghouse@gmail.com
sales@discoverypublishinggroup.com
web: www.discoverypublishinggroup.com

Printed at:
Infinity Imaging Systems
Delhi

PREFACE

The HIV/AIDS is a new phenomenon in the human society. HIV destroys the immune system of human individuals, producing a defenselessness fatal state known as AIDS. The World Health Organisation has estimated that already one in every two hundred and fifty adults in the world is infected with Human Immunodeficiency Virus and according to WHO's projections a total of forty million men women and children worldwide will have been infected with HIV by the turn of this twentieth century. Visualising the devastating effects of the HIV/AIDS epidemic within our life times and beyond is difficult. Probably, no other disease in recent times has had the impact on human society generated by HIV/AIDS.

The HIV/AIDS epidemic has brought into focus many health related ethical, legal and human rights issues. This epidemic requires immediate and effective responses in new programming areas: attitudinal and behavioural changes, community-based care and support initiatives, and the maintenance of human development in the face of increasing rates of illness and deaths. At this point, education enters the scene as it can alter the HIV/AIDS situation since it brings change in the behaviour of the people.

This *International Encyclopaedia of AIDS* presents the worldwide information about HIV/AIDS, issues and challenges, reports and reviews, ethics laws and human rights, and educational activities and programmes to keep the policy makers, planners, professionals, activists, researchers, educationists, teachers and students well informed of the epidemic.

Dr. Digumarti Bhaskara Rao
26 January 1999
The Republic Day of India

ACKNOWLEDGEMENT

I am thankful to the World Health Organisation and its associated offices for using their material namely School Health Education to prevent AIDS and STD: A Resource Package for Curriculum Planners-Handbook for Curriculum Planners. Student's Activities, Teachers' Guide, Global Programme on AIDS-HIV Prevention and Care: Teaching Modules for Nurses and Midwives, Global Programme on AIDS. Community HIV Prevention Handbook; STD care Management-workbooks 1-7, Facing the Challenge of HIV/AIDS/STDs: A Gender-based Response; HIV/AIDS and STD surveillance Data Management and Use-Report, Bangkok, 1995; Carrying out HIV Sentinal Surveillance-A Guide for Programme Managers, AIDS Prevention and Care in the workplace: Enhancing the Role of Private Sector; HIV Testing Policies and Guidelines; Carrying out HIV Sentinel surveillance; AIDS Prevention; Understanding and Living with AIDS; AIDS: A Modern Epidemic; HIV/AIDS in South-East Asia: IXth meeting of the National Programme Managers, New Delhi, 1993; Information, Education and Communication: A Guide for AIDS Programme Managers, Handbook on AIDS Home Care; HIV/AIDS in South-East Asia: A Pictorial summary; etc.

I am thankful to the United Nations Development Programme, UNDP's HIV and Development Programme, and UNDP's Regional Projects on HIV and Development for using their material namely Economic Implications of AIDS in Asia; Socio Economic Implications of the Epidemic; NGOs Working with Sex workers; NGO Responses to HIV/AIDS in Asia-Case Studies; HIV in the Workplace: Dealing with the Issues-Role Plays, Development and the HIV Epidemic, Law Ethics and HIV; HIV Law and Law Reform; Issue Papers; Study Papers; Working Papers; etc.

I am thankful to the Health and Nutrition Centre, Republic of Philippines for using its material namely sourcebook on HIV/AIDS Prevention Education for Tertiary Educational Institutions.

I am thankful to the Curriculum Development Programme, Ministry of Education, Government of Thailand for using its material namely Institutional Modules for AIDS Education.

I am thankful to US Department of Health and Human Services: Whitman-Walker Clinic, Inc., USA; East-West Centre, USA; National AIDS Control Organisation, Government of India; Academy of Culture Communication Education Science and Service, Guntur, United Nations and its agencies for using their material.

I am grateful to Bhaskar Bhattacharji; V. Alexeev, Geeta Sethi, Elizabeth Reid, Mina Mauerstein-Bail, A. A. Trinidad, Palomi Cuchi, D. Pushpa Latha for their kind co-operation.

Dr. Digumarti Bhaskara Rao,
Secretary
ACCESS
D-43, S.V. N. Colony,
Guntur-522 006

CONTENTS

Preface V
Acknowledgement VII

1. Instructor's Guide 1
2. Epidemiology and Transmission of HIV 9
3. HIV Infection and HIV-Related Illness 17
4. Prevention of HIV Transmission in Health Care Settings 27
5. The Psychological Impact of HIV Infection on the Individual and the Community 39
6. Developing Counselling Skills 47
7. Patient Education 54
8. Nursing Care of the Adult with HIV-Related Illness 65
9. The Impact of HIV Infection and HIV-Related Illness on Women 73
10. Nursing Care of the HIV Infant or Child with HIV-Related Illness 82
11. Terminal Care in HIV-Related Illness 91
12. Education of Traditional Practitioners to Prevent HIV Transmission through Skin-Piercing Practices 98
13. WHO Counselling Guidelines for HIV Testing 102
14. Consensus Statement from the WHO/UNICEF Consultation on HIV Transmission and Breast-Feeding 113

INSTRUCTOR'S GUIDE

APPLICATION

The modules are designed as a basic nursing education course on HIV-related illness. They cover the basic knowledge and skills which nurses need in order to effectively and safely practise their profession.

The modules are consecutive, each one building upon the knowledge and skills described in the previous module. They can also be presented separately. The optimum class size is 20 to 30 students.

The modules are designed to be taught as part of the curriculum of a school of nursing or midwifery. However, the techniques and materials can be adapted for use in continuing education programmes.

The *Learning Activities,* which form part of each module, call for the use of an overhead projector, photocopied material for hand-outs, and a blackboard and chalk or large sheets of paper and marking pens. The presentations can be modified depending on the resources available.

STRUCTURE OF THE MODULES

The course is divided into 11 separate modules. Each module has been developed as an individual lesson, which will take a minimum of two hours to present. Certain modules may take four to five hours.

All nurses will need the information contained in modules 1 to 5, irrespective of their area of expertise or geographic location. Selection of additional modules will depend upon the situation of the country concerned and the need to address specific topics.

Each module comprises:

— a general objective
— specific objectives
— an introduction
— learning activities, incorporating lesson plans.

In addition, background information for the instructor is provided in each module.

The Learning Activities, subject content and teaching strategies are identified within each module. The implementation of strategies for teaching and related use of materials are given in further detail below. These strategies can be used as part of each module at the most relevant and applicable times.

Activities in which the material is presented by group might include a written critique by the observing members. However, it is principally through participation in class discussions after the presentation that skills (planning, problem-solving and teaching) are developed and utilized. The effectiveness of the teaching strategy and level of learning, can best be measured by the response of the class during discussions as well as by the quantity of material learned by the students. An alternative method of evaluation is to ask the students to write answers to written discussion questions or to write short essays. This could be done outside class hours.

The suggested content and learning activities have been limited to basic infornation. Nursing and midwifery schools might find it challenging to incorporate additional material in their curricula.

INSTRUCTOR TRAINING

The instructors who implement these modules may need training to familiarize them with the content. This also provides an opportunity to develop their skill in facilitating the learning activities, many of which involve discussions and exercises addressing the highly charged and sensitive issues posed by HIV infection.

TEACHING STRATEGIES

An important feature of the modules is the use of interactive teaching strategies, allowing instruction, practice and feedback to take place. This approach is considered crucial in addressing the sensitive issues raised by the HIV pandemic. The various teaching strategies that are used are:

A. visual aids
B. board
C. presentation
D. large group discussions
E. small group discussions
F. role-play
G. case studies
H. fact finding
I. project work
J. questions.

A. Visual AIDS

— board or large sheets of paper
— photocopied material given to the students before the lecture
— transparencies used with an overhead projector
— slides and a slide projector
— reference for further studies
— video
— posters
— photographs.

B. The Board (or large sheets of paper)

The board is useful for outlining the learning activity. During the lesson, key points can be noted on the board and questions for debate or discussion (and responses) can be written on the board. The use of the board in this way promotes group discussion and interaction and allows feedback and evaluation to be appropriately structured and all writing must be clear and readable. The board should not be filled with too much details.

C. Presentation

The presentation is used to give information. During the presentation, the instructor can display key points or an outline on the board or transparencies while they talk to the students. Instructors can promote group interaction by the use of partially completed handouts which students can complete, by encouraging questions from the group following the presentation, by group work to discuss and answer questions or by assigning issues or tasks to small groups. From group discussions, the instructor can develop a list of points made which can be used to summarize the presentation.

Each presentation is followed by an activity which gives the students an opportunity to think critically about the information (e.g., group discussion). This will help each student to apply what has been learned to their own work situation.

D. Large Group Discussions

These should be led by the instructor and should involve the entire class. The advantages of such discussions include:

- the students provide information and become more confident because they have already acquired some knowledge
- the students are involved in problem-solving
- the students become active participants, which stimulates interest and motivates learning
- the learning process becomes more personal, requiring the instructor to take notes and comment upon individual opinions and ideas. This emphasizes important points (e.g., dealing with the misconception that HIV infection is spread by mosquitoes).
- the instructor is able to evaluate the students' understanding and absorption of material presented in class.

Large group discussions require a skilful instructor, who:

- asks questions or suggests topics, and directs the discussion to keep it relevant to the lesson's objectives
- may use transparencies on an overhead projector, or large paper or the board to promote interaction by writing up key questions or topics for discussion for each learning activity
- needs to ensure that all group members have equal opportunities to participate and that no one person (including the instructor) dominates the discussion
- needs to be flexible as the students may begin exploring another important issue
- is respectful and non judgemental of the students' ideas and opinions in order to allow for open expression of concerns
- keeps to time, leaving adequate periods for discussion
- obtains feedback and responses from the class to provide evaluation mechanisms for the lesson.

E. Small Group Discussions

These are organized in groups of 4 to 8. Students in small groups should be from a variety of backgrounds and job skills to enable a range of opinions on the given topic.

Some of the advantages of such discussions are:

- students have more opportunity to talk and are less likely to be embarrassed than if they were in a large group
- the atmosphere is more conducive to a discussion of feelings by students
- students gain self-confidence through sharing information
- they participate in problem-solving and improve their skills in this area.

The instructor does not lead the group, but must be skilful in structuring the discussions so that the students accomplish the stated objectives. Discussion questions or topics must be very clear. Rules must be set at the beginning of the discussion, for example:

- Which topics are to be discussed?
- Will the group draw conclusions or make decisions?
- Are the opinions or feelings of students private?
- Will the group be expected to report its discussion to the class?
- How much time does the group have?

The instructor may also:

— ask the group to appoint the following:
Chairman (to keep the group discussion focused on the topic)
— Time-keeper (to keep the group to time)
Secretary (to document the discussion)
Reporter (to present the findings)
— circulate between groups to monitor group activities and to assist as necessary
— Mdicate to the groups to begin concluding their discussions 5-10 minutes before time is up.

Small group discussions should be followed by a large group discussion so that general conclusions can be drawn.

F. Role-play

Role-play activities can be organized so that students play the parts of identified people and act out a scene. This is useful when practising skills such as counselling, and for exploring how people feel and react in specific situations. Role-plays could also be done by everyone at the same time (the class pairs off or divides into groups). Role-play has the following advantages:

— allows for safe rehearsal of skills and activities and provides good preparation for genuine situations
— students are involved in active participation and observation
— the actors are able to experience activities or interactions and not just discuss them in theory
— students are able to enhance their skills in observation and problem-solving
— allows for full expression and interpretation of concepts
— the instructor to evaluate the students' understanding of the topic.

Some students may feel intimidated by role-playing. The instructor must be skilful in ensuring that they feel relaxed and should:

— keep the role-play friendly and informal
— emphasize that the characters are "in role" and that group

observers are looking at the character and their reactions, not at the people playing them

- set up the role-play situation, showing how interaction ought to take place to familiarize the group to the process; this "warms up" the class and gives the actors a chance to practise
- ask for volunteers instead of assigning roles to people.

The instructor should be one of the first actors.

Implementing role-play:

- Two or more people role-play before one or a group of observers

  The role-play situation should be detailed and realistic
- All players must be clear about the character they are meant to become (clue cards may be provided to outline the role and the present problem)
- Actors never use their own name in role-play situations
- Each player acts out the role spontaneously without prior preparation, i.e., "puts himself into the other person's shoes"
- Encourage the players to be creative and imaginative
- There is no prescription or prohibition of behaviour
- Instructors must not interrupt or interfere during the role-play
- Allow time to enable actors to "get into role" but keep it as brief as possible.

AT THE END OF ROLE-PLAYING

This approach to small group teaching can become charged with emotion. Bringing people "out" of their roles is of paramount importonce, otherwise negative or hostile feelings may persist, causing continued discomfort and anxiety.

Techniques for doing this include:

- engaging in discussion of a totally unrelated topic to promote interaction thut brings the group back to the "here and now".
- allowing further discussion of any issue of concern.
- allowing objective feedback on aspects of the portrayal of the roles and how real the situation felt
- asking actors and observers what they liked about the interaction and what might have been done differently
- asking the class what they leamt from the role-play
- drawing the class's attention back to the objectives, or to the main points that the role-play was to demonstrote. For example. if the objective was to practise counselling a person with HIV infection, whut are the points to remember?

G. Case Studies

Cas studies are an excellent way to give students an understanding of the effect of HIV infection on the individual, and to enable them to deal with problems they may encounter in a health care setting. The instructor is recommended to develop case studies that are specific to the work setting in which the students will practice. Examples of case studies are suggested in the modules.

The advantages of case studies are that they:
- facilitate the active involvement of the students
- allow an examination of a real or simulated problem that mirrors the outside world
- allow students to identify underlying general principles
- develop confidence, and an understanding of complex issues
- may be used in role-play or problem-solving exercises

Case studies include both short vignettes (descriptions of situations, stories) and longer descriptions. Usually, questions are asked that address an objective in the module concerned. These questions may be discussed in small groups or with the entire class. The responses of the students also provide a method for evaluating of this particular Learning Activity .

H. Fact-finding

Fact-finding teaches the students to locate information on their own. This is a good way to discover resources and interact with people in the community. It has the following advantages:
- students experience meeting people, seeing facilities, and going into health care settings
- they are active participants in the learning process
- they are involved in problem-solving and observation
- they gain self-confidence in their role in the health care setting.

The instructor must identify precisely what information the students need to collect.

The students can write reports about their experience or report verbally to the class. Presentations and group discussions are very useful, as students will learn from each other's experience as well as their own.

I. Project Work

Project work brings together the experiences of the students. It may be carried out by an individual or by small groups.

The instructor:
- needs to ensure that the main purpose is explained and clarified before the project is undertaken
- might write out lists of relevant questions on the board or on large pieces of paper or on handouts
- may give different questions to different groups.

Advantages of project work include:

- encourages active participation of the students
- fosters cooperation
- develops confidence in obtaining relevant data
- develops confidence in making decisions
- enables students to recognize and assess what they have learned from the process
- presentation of the project enables evaluation of learning.

J. Questions

Questions, both verbal and written, are used in many of the strategies throughout the modules. They provide a valuable means of ongoing evaluation and further involve the students in their own learning.

Techniques include:

- constructing questions so that more than one answer is possible
- saying as little as possible
- giving clues to encourage responses
- using good listening skills encouraging non-verbal clues
- using clear and unambiguous wording
- pausing after asking a question
- allowing students time for compiling and reflecting on answers
- prompting to help students further their awareness without giving too much away.

SUMMARY

To help the instructor, each module contains:

- Background information, giving important factual information related to the topic
- Learning activities, designed to help students achieve the objectives of each module.
- Teaching guidelines, to suggest ways in which each of the learning activities can be implemented.

Note: The next chapters constitute the modules of this package-HIV prevention and care: Teaching Modules for Nurses and Midwives.

EPIDEMIOLOGY AND TRANSMISSION OF HIV

GENERAL OBJECTIVE

On completion of this module, the student will be able to apply a knowledge of basic epidemiology and an understanding of how HIV is transmitted to their role in preventing further spread of infection.

SPECIFIC OBJECTIVES

On completion of this module, the student should be able:

- to identify personal and community fears and worries about HIV infection
- to explain how *HIV is* and *is not* transmitted
- to describe the role of the nurse in preventing the spread of HIV infection in the community
- to discuss the local, as well as the national and global epidemiological aspects of the AIDS pandemic, including the importance of national surveillance in understanding and responding to HIV infection in the community
- to describe ways in which information can be collected to help identify the demographic characteristics and risk behaviours of people reported to be infected with HIV.

INTRODUCTION

HIV infection is a condition which generates fear and misunderstanding. Being part of the community, nurses are likely to share the same fears and misconceptions as other members of the community. It is essential, therefore, for nurses to have a clear understanding of their own fears and concerns; only then will it be possible to separate the unfounded fears from the real. Nurses need to understand the scope of the AIDS pandemic and how HIV is transmitted. This is the first step in preparing them to be informed professionals with the expertise needed to address the problems of HIV infection.

LEARNING ACTIVITIES

Learning Activities Key *(Module 1)*

Learning Activity 1	Identify Personal and Community Fears and Anxieties
Learning Activity 2	Transmission of HIV
Learning Activity 3	Local, National and Global Epidemiology
Learning Activity 4	Collecting Data and Identifying Local Surveillance Resources

Learning Activity 1: is important in the educational process because it encourages students to explore the fears and myths associated with HIV infection. The opportunity to examine personal fears helps them to separate the facts they learn from any unfounded fears they may have about HIV infection.

Learning Activity 2: introduces epidemiological information on HIV transmission. The students examine the myths identified in *LearningActivity 1* and compare them with actual information about HIV transmission . They participate in, or evaluate, a role-play of a nurse explaining to a person how HIV is and is not transmitted. This enables students to think of their educational role in the community and to identify any questions they may have about transmission.

Learning Activity 3: introduces the local, as well as the national and global, epidemiological picture of HIV infection. This information is used to present the concept of epidemiological surveillance. Nurses need to know how people may become infected in their communities and what the major risk factors are. These may differ in each community.

Learning Activity 4: requires the students to collect data specific to their own community and country. Students are assigned to find information and to report back to the class. If *Modules I* and 3 are taught in different classes, the activity can be implemented entirely within *Module 1,* with students reporting to the class at the next class period. If *Modules* I and 3 are taught within one class, the students can report their findings at the beginning of *Module* 3, as the information collected is necessary to meet the objectives of this module. If there is insufficient time or resources for the students to find the information, the instructor can use the list provided in *Learning Activity* 4 as a basis for the information presented to the class.

Learning Activity 1 IDENTIFY PERSONAL AND COMMUNITY FEARS AND ANXIETIES

It may be helpful to introduce this exercise with a few preparatory remarks. For example:

"Many of us are afraid when we first hear the word AIDS. Opinions differ about what the disease is, how it is spread, who gets it and how many people die of the illness. Let us begin our study of HIV infection and AIDS by looking at what you already know, how you feel and what other people in your community think and feel about AIDS."

Write the following questions on the board or on a large sheet of paper:

- What have you heard about HIV infection and AIDS?
- Describe the different ways that people in your community say that HIV infection is spread.
- How do you think HIV infection is spread?
- When you think about providing care for a person with AIDS, what is your reaction?

Divide the class into smaller groups and allow 15 to 20 minutes for discussion. Ask the students if anyone would like to share the group's answers with the class. As you facilitate the discussion, acknowledge the fears and worries which the students may have and also note the various ideas which they have heard expressed about AIDS in their community. Write these responses on a blackboard or large piece of paper under the headings, "How people feel about people with AIDS" and "How people think AIDS is spread".

Learning Activity 2 TRANSMISSION OF HIV

Students will need the following Background Information to understand how scientists came to discover the cause of AIDS, and how the virus which causes this disease is transmitted.

Background Information

The disease that we now call AIDS was first recognized in countries in the developed world (e.g., United States of America, Australia, New Zealand, and in Europe) among male homosexuals in the early 1980s. In other countries, AIDS was diagnosed primarily in heterosexual men and women. Because AIDS was affecting individuals who were sexually active, scientists concluded that the cause was probably a sexually transmitted microbe.

As scientists continued to study the disease, it was observed that many cases also occurred among:

- injecting drug users
- recipients of blood transfusions,
  and,
- children and adults with haemophilia.

The factor that these people had in common was that all had received blood or blood products many injecting drug users share the same injecting equipment).
Babies were also found to have this disease because their mothers had been infected. This indicated perinatal transmission.
Following further scientific studies, the transmission pattern for the infective agent became evident. Only people who were sexually active, or who had received injections of someone else's blood or who were born to infected mothers, developed the disease.
When these facts became known, scientists concluded that AIDS was caused by a blood-borne microbe, probably a virus, which was transmitted to sexual partners, or to people who had received blood or blood products, as well as to the unborn or newly born babies of infected mothers.
In 1983 the virus that caused AIDS was discovered by scientists in France and the routes of transmission were confirmed. This virus eventually became known as the human immunodeficiency virus HIV). We now know that there are at lest two different major types of this virus, one called HIV- 1 and the other known as HIV-2. HIV-1 is the principal AIDS virus while HIV-2 is found mainly in West African countries. Scientists also studied thousands of people living or working with people who had developed AIDS. They found that it was only the sexual partners of infected individuals who became infected and subsequently developed AIDS. From this it became clear that HIV infection is not acquired by casual social contact.

Prepare important points from the above presentation on transparencies or handouts for the class, in advance. Alternatively, ask one of the students to write this information onto large pieces of paper or on the board while you are doing the presentation, leaving the information from *Learning Activity I* on display. While presenting this information, encourage students to ask questions.

Divide students into groups and have them list:

— different ways in which HIV can be transmitted;
— ways in which HIV is not transmitted.

Allow them 15 to 20 minutes to make their lists and then bring the group back together. In large group discussion, ask for contributions from each group and have the students construct a "Summary List" on the board or on large pieces of paper. Here is an example of a "Summary List".

Example of Summary List:

HIV TRANSMISSION

- HIV CAN BE TRANSMITTED:

    - Sexually, through intercourse or through contact with infected blood, semen, or cervical and vaginal fluids. This is the most frequent mode of transmission and HIV can be transmitted from any infected person to his or her sexual partner (man to woman, woman to man, man to man and, but less likely, woman to woman).

- During transfusion of blood or blood products obtained from donor blood infected with HIV;
- Using injecting or skin-piercing equipment contaminated with HIV.
- From a mother infected with HIV to her child during pregnancy, during labour, or following birth as a result of breast-feeding.

• HIV CANNOT BE TRANSMITTED BY:

- Coughing or sneezing
- Handshakes
- Insect bites
- Work or school contacts
- Touching or hugging
- Using toilets
- Water or food
- Using telephones
- Kissing
- Swimming pools
- Public baths
- Sharing cups, glasses, plates and other eating and drinking utensils.

From the above list it can be seen that the most common method of being infected with HIV is from sexual intercourse and today most individuals who have become infected have done so as a result of heterosexual exposure to the virus.

It is important to stress at this point that in the great majority of work activities, nurses are not at risk of becoming infected by people with whom they work.

Finally, summarize the important facts which you have covered so far, such as:

Important Facts

- AIDS is caused by a virus called the human immunodeficiency virus (HIV).
- People who are infected with HIV often have no symptoms of disease for many years and can, therefore, infect others without realising that they themselves are infected.
- AIDS refers to specific clinical manifestations seen during the later part of HIV infection when people are ill as a result of this infection.
- By mid-1993, 2.5 million people including half a million children) are estimated by WHO to have reached the later stages of HIV infection known as AIDS. In addition to the people who have AIDS, WHO estimates that over 11.5 million men, women and children have been infected with HIV.
- Most, if not all, individuals infected with HIV will eventually develop AIDS. The average time between HIV infection and the onset of AIDS is approximately 10 years for HIV-1, and around 17 years for HIV-2. In both cases, this period may be significantly shorter in developing countries where nutritional status may be low and access to effective treatment limited, and is much shorter in children with HIV infection.

- Although many of the opportunistic diseases seen in AIDS can be managed, there is presently no cure for AIDS. According to our present knowledge, most people with AIDS will eventually die of the disease.
- Although scientists all over the world are working on developing a vaccine to prevent HIV infection, it may be many years before one is available. Prevention is only possible at present through education, and nurses have an important, if not critical, role to play in teaching their patients and fellow citizens how HIV is and is not transmitted, and how people can protect themselves against infection.

After summarizing the above information, ask the class to review the list of ways people think HIV is spread from *Learning Activity I* and to identify those that are correct and those that are incorrect.

Then, have students divide into small groups and in each group have two students role-play the following scenario:

"A nurse is out shopping and meets a neighbour who tells her that she is afraid to drink the water because she has heard she may get AIDS that way. The nurse explains to her how HIV infection is spread. The neighbour continues to offer arguments such as those identified in learning Activity 1."

Allow 10 minutes for the role-play, then ask each group to report what it learnt from the exercise. Ask the students to identify any issues that they are still unsure about and answer any questions that they may have.

Learning Activity 3 LOCAL, NATIONAL AND GLOBAL EPIDEMIOLOGY

Using local references, present information on the incidence and prevalence of HIV infection and AIDS in your own community. Present this information on transparencies or large pieces of paper.

Using WHO references, present information on the incidence and prevalence of HIV infection and AIDS nationally and throughout the world.

Facilitate class discussion and participation as you talk by asking the discussion questions included in the following Background Information.

Background Information

Incidence means the "number of times an event occurs in a given time e.g., the number of new AIDS cases presenting each month or the number of new HIV infections being detected during a specified period of time. Prevalence means "the total number of specific conditions in existence in a defined population at a precise point in times." e.g., the number of AIDS cases or number of HIV infections which have so far been reported in your own country. The systematic collection of facts (data) about disease occurrence is called surveillance. It is very important to learn about AIDS and HIV infection in every country through notional surveillance programmes. Only then can an answer be found to some of the following questions:

- How many people in your local community are now infected with HIV? (prevalence)
- How is HIV being transmitted in your own country?
- What is the rate of new HIV infections in your own country? (incidence)
- How mony AIDS cases have so far been reponred in your own country (prevalence)?
  [Knowing this information assists in planning interventions to help prevent the further spread of HIV infection, e.g., by allocating resources (people, time and money) to health education, testing and the provision of clinical services.]
- What would you like to know about the HIV epidemic in your country?
- What information would help you as a nurse?

Learning Activity 4 COLLECTING DATA ON HIV INFECTION

In this Learning Activity, the students collect, if it is available, information about the local demographics of HIV infection, the system of surveillance in their own country, the resources available for prevention, education, counselling and the clinical care of people with HIV infection and AIDS.

If there is no time to do the data collection, the instructor can use the questions in this Learning Activity to structure his or her own information on this important topic. The information pertaining to the following questions can form the basis of an introductory review in *Module 3.*

Have each student choose a partner with whom to do this project. The tasks are to find the answers to as many of the following questions as possible. List these questions on the board or hand them out on paper.

An alternative would be to assign questions 1-4 to some groups and questions 5-10 to others, as the sources of information for the first four questions may be different from those for the remaining questions.

Divide the students into pairs or small groups and arrange for them to visit staff at the services listed below. The purpose of the visit is to help the students collect the data required to answer the following questions, and to make them feel confident that they can access relevant data in the future.

Arrange Visits To:

- The National AIDS Programme
- Health centres involved in testing or counselling people
- Hospitals caring for people with HIV with HIV infection or AIDS
- STD services
- Blood Transfusion Service - Any other facility where data related to HIV infection or AIDS is collected or where people may go to access HIV-related services.

Questions:

1. Having visited one of the above facilities, what kind of HIV/AIDS surveillance is being conducted (e.g., sentinel surveillance of HIV, number of new AIDS cases, etc.)?
2. Who is doing HIV antibody testing in your local community? Is pre- and post-test counselling available and if so, what kind of training have the counsellors had?
3. Where can people with AIDS be cared for in your local community? How are people referred to these facilities and what services are offered?
4. What social services are available for people with HIV infection or AIDS and who provides them? Is there a programme to provide home-based care for people with AIDS?
5. Is AIDS a reportable (notifiable) disease in your country? If so, who reports (e.g., doctors, nurses), and to whom? Is there a special form for reporting and if so what information does this form require? Obtain a copy of this form for the rest of the class to see.
6. What is the total number of people in your country who have so far been reported to have AIDS? What percentage is this of the total population?
7. How many HIV antibody tests have been done in your country in the last year and of this total, how many were positive? How did this compare with the number of tests done last year and the number of positive results at that time?
8. From available data, describe the major transmission categories in your own country (e.g., hetrosexual, homosexual, injecting drug use, blood transfusion recipient.
9. How are AIDS cases and/or people with positive HIV antibody test results distributed with regard to age, sex, region and risk behaviours? How is this information collected?
10. How does the prevalence and incidence of AIDS and HIV infection compare in your country with other selected countries?

HIV INFECTION AND HIV-RELATED ILLNESS

GENERAL OBJECTIVE

On completion of this module, the student will have a broad understanding of the clinical consequences of HIV infection and will be able to discuss the rationale for voluntary, anonymous or unlinked testing for HIV infection.

SPECIFIC OBJECTIVES

On completion of this module, the student should be able:

- to explain how HIV affects the immune system
- to recognise the national definition of AIDS
- to recognise symptomatic HIV infections
- to describe the clinical course and staging of HIV infection
- to identify situations in which HIV antibody testing is appropriate and beneficial.

INTRODUCTION

This module will consolidate learning already achieved in *Module* 1 and will focus on facilitating an understanding of the clinical consequences of HIV infection. In addition, students will gain an understanding of the natural history of HIV infection and HIV-related illness and will be able to describe an appropriate classification (staging) system for this condition, applicable to their own country. The knowledge gained from both this module and *Module 1* will form the basis for:

— health education and primary prevention strategies
— counselling, in relation to voluntary serological testing for HIV antibodies, and clinical outcomes of HIV infection
— assessing, planning and implementing meaningful nursing interventions.

LEARNING ACTIVITIES

Learning Activities

Learning Activity 1	Basic Concepts: HIV Infection
Learning Activity 2	Natural History of HIV Infection
Learning Activity 3	Serological Testing for HIV Infection
Learning Activity 4	Defining *Terms*
Learning Activity 5	Differential Diagnosis in HIV Infection

Learning Activity 1 BASIC CONCEPTS: HIV INFECTION

Prior to this session, the instructor may find it useful to review with the class the normal basic functions of both the immune system and possibly the nervous system. Following this review, present the following *Background Information* to the class, either on the blackboard or as transparencies with an overhead projector.

Background Information

THE IMMUNE SYSTEM

The immune system is the body's defence against infections by microorganisms that have been able to get past the skin or the mucous membranes and which can cause disease. The immune system produces antibodies to neutralize microorganisms and activates special blood cells which work to kill and remove these organisms from the body. When the immune system is not functioning as it should, the person is described as having an immunodeficiency. HIV infects special cells in the immune system called lymphocytes (T4 helper cells) and monocytes, eventually destroying these cells. This slowly leads to a persistent, progressive and profound impairment of the immune system, making an individual susceptible to infections and conditions such as cancer.

There are other causes of either temporary or permanent immunodeficiency, including:

— congenital defects in the immune system, i.e., primary immune dysfunction
— immune dysfunction secondary to drugs, e.g. those used in immunosuppressant therapy, or anti-cancer drugs; cancers; malnutrition; irradiation (both accidental and therapeutic); other infections, especially with other viruses.

THE NERVOUS SYSTEM

HIV infects both the central and peripheral nervous system early in the course of infection, causing a variety of neurological and neuropsychiatric conditions, in children and adults. In addition, the impairment of the immune system leaves the nervous system vulnerable to opportunistic infections and cancers.

OPPORTUNISTIC DISEASE

An opportunistic disease is one which normally would not be a problem because of the body's ability to control it with the immune system, but which can become a major problem when immunodeficiency occurs.
Consequently, opportunistic diseases occur only in individuals whose immune system is depressed.

There are many microorganisms that commonly inhabit the body without causing any illness, but when the immune system is depressed, they can cause serious problems. One example of an organism that causes an opportunistic disease is candida, a fungus found in the mouth of most people but rarely causing "thrush" unless the immune system is depressed and not able to control the growth of the oral candida. Pneumocystis carinii, which is found in the lungs of people without causing any illness, causes pneumonia in people with immunodeficiency. The tubercle bacillus (*Mycobacterium tuberculosis*), also commonly found in the lungs, can re-activate when the immune system is depressed, causing pulmonary tuberculosis, a common opportunistic infection seen in people with HIV Infection. Another common example in Africa is Cryptococcus neoformans (also known as *Filobasidiella* neoformans) which can cause meningitis in an immunodeficient person.

Allow 20 minutes for open discussion, supplying additional information, as needed, on how HIV infection damages both the immune and nervous systems and clarifying the concept of opportunistic diseases.

Learning Activity 2 NATURAL HISTORY OF HIV INFECTION

Once again, present the following *Background Information* to the class, using the blackboard or transparencies on an overhead projector.

Background Information

HIV INFECTION

HIV infection progresses through several stages. It begins when an individual becomes infected with the virus, as described in Module 1. As described in Learning Activity 1, HIV infection causes a progressive impirment of both the immune and nervous systems. Cher time, as this impairment worsens, it begins to show itself as symptoms.. Consequently, there are various stages in the sequence of increasingly serious consequences of HIV infection. The early, middle and late manifestations of HIV infection can therefore be classified. In addition, once infected, the person is infectious (i.e., able to transmit the virus to other people) for life.

ACUTE *SEROCONVERSION ILLNESS*

Within three to eight weeks after infection, some (but not all) people develop an acute illness lasting two to three weeks with symptoms such as fevers, rash, joint and muscle pain, swollen lymph glands, diarrhoea and sore throat. Symptoms may be mild and will eventually disappear completely. This self-limiting condition is known as an acute seroconversion illness. During this period the virus continues to reproduce itself inside the body and the person's immune system responds by developing antibodies to the virus. Within six to twelve weeks after infection, it is usually possible to detect HIV antibodies in the blood. Unlike antibodies to most other microorganisms, these antibodies do not destroy the virus effectively. In some infected people, antibodies cannot be detected for six months or longer, yet they are still infected and infectious.

ASYMPTOMATIC INFECTION

The person may remain asymptomatic and feel and appear healthy for years, even though he or she is infected with HIV. During this asymptomatic period, the person remains infectious (i.e., able to transmit the virus to others via sexual, blood-borne and perinatal transmission) and, as the virus continues to replicate, progressive damage to both the immune and nervous systems result over time. If their blood is tested during this stage it will test positive for HIV antibodies. Some individuals will have persistently enlarged lymph nodes (persistent generalized lymph aenopathy or PGL) during the asymptomatic stage of HIV infection.

EARLY SYMPTOMATIC ILLNESS

Many individuals eventually develop a variety of indicators of ill health due to HIV infection without developing AIDS-defining opportunistic infections or secondary cancers. These constitutional symptoms and signs are sometimes referred to as the AIDS-related Complex (ARC) . These symptoms include complaints such as oral thrush, diarrhoea, weight loss, low-grade intermittent fevers and night sweats, a variety of skin rashes, loss of energy, etc. Various fungal diseases (e.g., tinea infections) or viral diseases (e.g. shingles) may be seen and individuals feel chronically ill during this stage of HIV infection.

LATE SYMPTOMATIC ILLNESS, i.e. AIDS

Eventually, individuals will have episodes of AIDS-specific opportunistic diseases, such as *Pneulrxvstis canniipneurnonia, encephalitis* caused by *Toxoplasmagonda*, and severe and *chronic diarrtioea causedby cryptosporijia* and *microsporidia*. Pulmonary tuberculosis is increasingly being recognized as one of the most common opportunistic diseases associated with HIV infection, especially in the developing world. Opportunistic cancers such as *Kaposi sarcoma* and undifferentiated B-cell lymphomas may also be seen. In addition to the above, there will be significant weight loss and both neurological and neuropsychiatric syndromes may be present. This end stage of HIV infection is referred to as AIDS. Patients in this stage will eventually enter a terminal phase and die (see Module 10).

Following this presentation, ask students to describe the clinical picture of people infected with HIV whom they have nursed, or of the case studies described below, and relate these various case descriptions to the above stages of HIV infection. With the available information in the case studies, ask the students to decide on how these cases are to be classified and what is the likely clinical outcome for each case. Allow 20 minutes for this discussion and then have each group report back to the class.

Many countries have adopted their own definition of AIDS, based on one or more of the case definitions available. For nurses who need to recognise symptomatic HIV infection for purposes of clinical management, for a simple overview of HIV associated clinical findings.

If the students have access to a library or reference centre, you could ask them to see if they can find an AIDS case definition for themselves, so that they can compare definitions and see the differences and similarities by presenting the definition that they found to the rest of the group.

CASE STUDY 1

Mr. T. went to donate blood at the National Transfusion Centre but after a blood test he was told he was HIV positive and couldn't donate blood anymore. He is somewhat confused as he feels quite well.

CASE STUDY 2

Mrs. A. has been unwell for several months, with diarrhoea. She has been tested previously and is known to be inflected with HIV. However, other than diarrhoea, her only other complaint is that she always feels tired and unwell.

CASE STUDY 3

Mr. W. is unwell, complaining of chronic diarrhoea and fever for the last 7 weeks and a persistent cough for the last five weeks. He also has had oral thrush for the last several weeks.

Learning Activity 3 SEROLOGICAL TESTING FOR HIV INFECTION

Introduce this Learning Activity by presenting the following background information to the class, using either a blackboard, large sheets of paper or transparencies on an overhead projector.

Testing for HIV Antibodies

Any blood test used to detect HIV infection must have a high degree of sensitivity (the probability that the test will be positive if the patient is infected) and specificity (the probability that the test will be negative if the patient is uninfected). No antibody test is ever 100 per cent sensitive and specific and, therefore, all positive test results should be confirmed by testing, preferably by a different test method, if available. HIV antibody tests usually become positive within 3 months of the individual being infected with the virus. However, in some individuals, the test may not be positive until 6 months or longer (although this would be considered unusual).

FALSE POSITIVE RESULT

HIV tests have been developed to be especially sensitive and, conseaquently, a positive result will sometimes be obtained even when there are no HIV antibodies in the blood . This is known as a false positive, and because of this all positive results must be confirmed by another test method. A confirmed positive result means that the individual is infected with HIV.

FALSE NEGATIVE RESULT

This situation occurs when the blood tested gives a negative result for HIV antibodies when, in fact, it should really have been positive, as the person is infected. The iikelihood of a false negative test result must be discussed with patients if their history suggests that they have engaged in behaviour which was likely to put them at risk of HIV infecti n. In this situation, repeated testing over time maybe necessary before they can be reassured that they are not infected with HIV. The most frequent reason that a false negative test result has been obtained is that the individual is newly infected and is not yet producing HIV antibodies. However, it is important to remember that someone who has tested negative because they are not infected with HIV, can become infected the following day!

Conclude this presentation by emphasizing the following:

> *All patients must give informed consent prior to being tested for HIV antibodies, the results of their test (and the fact that they were tested) must be kept absolutely confidential and the patient must have both pre-and post-test counselling (see Module 5 and Chapter 13).*

Now, have the students discuss the following questions in small groups and then report back to the class. Allow 45; minutes for this activity.

Discussion Questions

1. Why is it important not to have false negative results during the testing of blood that is to be used for transfusions?
2. Why is it important to have a positive test confirmed?
3. Why is it necessary to have the individual's informed consent prior to this test?
4. Why is it necessary to keep the test results confidential?
5. Some people would like to test everyone for HIV antibodies. Is this useful?

Conclude this session by answering any questions and clarifying any issues raised by the class.

Learning Activity 4 DEFINING TERMS

Ask the class to define the following terms using a simple brainstorming technique.

• IMMUNE SYSTEM

A complex system which includes lymphoid related tissues such as the bone marrow, thymus, spleen, tonsils, adenoids, appendix, Peyer's patches, lymph nodes and blood and lymphatic vessels. Exposure to bacteria, viruses, fungi, parasites, harmful food substances or environmental toxins induces a response in the cells and secretions of the immune system, most notably the lymphocytes, phagocytes and antibodies.

• IMMUNODEFICIENCY

Describes the condition where a person's immune system cannot protect the body, resulting in an increased susceptibility to various infections and cancers.

• OPPORTUNISTIC DISEASES

Diseases that take advantage of the body's lowered resistance, due to the destruction of the immune system by HIV. These may be infections, such as *pneumocystis carinii pneumonia, toxoplasmosis encephalitis, or cancers,* such as *Kaposi sarcoma.*

• HIV

Human (because the microorganism attacks humans) *Immunodeficiency* {the microorganism causes damage to the immune system) Virus (the microorganism is a virus).

• ASYMPTOMATIC HIV INFECTION

The person is infected with HIV but has no symptoms. He or she can spread the virus to others by sexual intercourse, perinatally or through blood. HIV transmission can also occur during the symptomatic phase of HIV infection and when a person has AIDS.

• SYMPTOMATIC HIV INFECTION

The person is infected with HIV and has some symptoms (e.g., diarrhoea, fever, or malaise), but does not meet the criteria for a diagnosis of AIDS to be made.

• AIDS

Acquired (transmitted from person to person) *Immunodeficiency (impairment* of the body's ability to fight infections and certain cancers) Syndrome (a collection of signs and symptoms).

Learning Activity 5 DIFFERENTIAL DIAGNOSIS IN HIV INFECTION

This final Learning Activity is optional and is included to cover those situations in which nursing personnel are involved in establishing the medical diagnosis. However, in most nursing environments, making a medical diagnosis is usually the role of a physician, not a nurse.

Present the following information before leading an exercise comparing the symptoms associated with HIV infection with symptoms of other diseases.

Diagnosis of HIV Infection

The symptoms of HIV infection and of the associated opportunistic diseases are often life-threatening. There is no cure for HIV infection but many of the opportunistic diseases can be treated. Nurses in a clinic or community health cure setting must be able to recognize the signs and symptoms in order to refer the person to a medical centre for possible diagnosis and treatment of these diseases.

In determining whether person has HIV infection, three factors must be considered:

1. Assessment of the clinical signs of the disease.
2. Result of the HIV antibody test.
   Although an HIV antibody test is not necessary for diagnosing a person, and is not helpful in treating the symptoms of opportunistic diseases, it can confirm the clinical impression, when positive, and speed up the diagnosis.
3. History-taking to determine possible risk behaviours or factors.
   This will be determined by knowledge of how HIV is transmitted locally. Below is a list of possible risk factors and behaviours:
   - High-risk exposure (e.g., through unprotected sexual intercourse, or sharing of skin-piercing equipment such as injection equipment)
   - Frequent sexual activity with multiple partners
   - Male homosexual or biaexual activities
   - Sexual intercourse with a person at high risk of HIV infection
   - Blood transfusions (in areas where the blood supply is tested for HIV, the major question would be whether transfusion occurred before the date when blood began to be tested)
   - Sharing needles during injecting drug use or other exposures to potentially unsterilized needles.

In localities where HIV infection is common, people with both Mycobacterium tuberculosis infection and HIV infection may also be found. Casual contact with a person with HIV infection will not result in others becoming infected with HIV. However, if this person also has tuberculosis, others are at risk of contracting tuberculosis.

Lead the class in a discussion comparing the symptoms of HIV infection with those of other diseases. Give specific disease examples which are common locally. Have the students compare symptoms and disease progression. Because of the similarities between AIDS and so many other disease processes, the clearest difference may be the long duration of the symptoms of AIDS.

The following cases are situations that the nurse may encounter in an outpatient setting. They are only suggestions and should be adapted by the instructor using the local language (for example, what words do people use for their sexual partners, husbands and wives?) and demographic characteristics of people with HIV infection.

Divide the class into small groups to discuss the examples. Tell them to spend five minute on each case. After half an hour, ask one group to report what they have decided about case number one; the other groups may provide any additional ideas. They should consider the following questions:

1. What additional information would be useful
2. What disease do you suspect and why

Case Studies

1. A woman has had progressive weight loss for six months. She is weak and has to sit down after walking to the clinic. She has a poor appetite and has had diarrhoea for the past five months. She comes from a village in which there has been a history of dysentery. She has had no fever, her lymph nodes are normal, and she has no cough.
2. A woman has a chronic cough, shortness of breath upon walking, and has had fever in the afternoon for the last six months. She eats poorly and is always tired. She has had several sexual partners in the past two years.
3. A man has swollen lymph nodes, fevers and night sweats, and has experienced weight loss for the last eight months. He has diarrhoea, says he has no appetite and feels a bad taste in his mouth. He has thick, white patches on his tongue. When asked about his sexual activity, he says he has been married for a year, but had many sexual partners before that.
4. A man has a dry cough, shortness of breath when walking, and feels exhausted by the afternoon every day. He has experienced a 5 kg weight loss in the last month and notices that his memory has been poor lately. You notice that his speech is slow and slightly slurred when he talks. When asked, he says he has sex with both women and men.
5. A mother brings her three-year old child into the health care centre because he is lethargic and his legs seem weak. His appetite is

poor and he has had diarrhoea and persistent fevers for one month. She says he was treated for leukaemia just a year ago, and she is worried that he is becoming sick with it again.

POSSIBLE ANSWERS

1. It is possible that this woman has intestinal parasites. All of her symptoms could be related to this diagnosis. A more complete physical examination would determine whether she has other symptoms possibly related to HIV. It would be a good idea to determine if she has possibly been exposed to HIV, by asking her if she or her partner has engaged in any of the risk behaviours (many sexual partners, injecting drug use), or if either of them has a history of blood transfusion. If she is treated for parasites and her poor condition continues, HIV infection should be suspected.
2. The woman could have tuberculosis. A chest X-ray and sputum test should be performed. It should be recalled that a person with HIV infection is susceptible to tuberculosis. She has engaged in sexual risk behaviour and is at risk for HIV infection. Referral for further diagnostic investigation is also recommended.
3. The man has many signs and symptoms associated with symptomatic HIV infection. The white patches could becaused by oral Candida infection, which is every common problem with HIV infection. He has also had many sexual partners, which puts him at risk of having been exposed to HIV.
4. The man has the signs and symptoms of HIV infection. Poor memory and slurred speech are the symptoms which distinguish his condition from that of possible tuberculosis (although he should, in fad, also be examined for tuberculosis).
5. Try to determine whether the symptoms are a result of recurrent enteritis or HIV infection. Ask the mother about possible risk factors. This will give an idea of whether HIV infection is likely. This includes the m others possible risk behaviours. For example, how many people has she had sex with? Has she ever used injecting drugs? Has she ever had a blood transfusion? Has her baby had a blood transfusion or many injections? What is the mother's state of health? And the father's?

PREVENTION OF HIV TRANSMISSION IN HEALTH CARE SETTINGS

GENERAL OBJECTIVE

On completion of this module, the student will be able to develop strategies for preventing HIV transmission in the health care setting and participate in nursing education activities designed to facilitate the implementation of universal infection control precautions into all aspects of clinical nursing practice.

SPECIFIC OBJECTIVES

On completion of this module, the student should be able:

- to identify possible ways in which HIV is transmitted in the health care setting
- to describe universal infection control precautions and the rationale for their use
- to describe precautions against accidental exposure to needles and sharp instruments
- to apply problem-solving skills in order to prevent exposure to HIV in the health care setting
- to identify alternatives for invasive or skin-piercing procedures in the health care setting
- to prepare other staff to integrate universal infection control precautions into their clinical practice.

INTRODUCTION

HIV (and other bloodborne pathogens, e.g. Hepatitis B virus) may be transmitted in the health care setting from patient to patient, from patient to health care worker or, more rarely, from health care worker to patient. In each of these forms of transmission, the risk depends on the prevalence of infected individuals in the population, the frequency of exposure to contaminated medical instruments, the nature of such exposures, the relative infectivity of the virus, and the concentration of the virus in the blood.

Since it is not practical or desirable to identify everyone who is infected with HIV, the strategy for preventing HIV transmission in the health care setting is to *view everyone as having the potential to be infected.* The only reason to focus on identified infected individuals is to provide counselling, support, treatment and care.

This module emphasizes the inclusion of universal precautions into current nursing practice, as recommended by both the International Council of Nurses and the World Health Organization. Health care facilities need to ensure that their universal precautions are consistent with national guidelines and with WHO and ICN recommendations.

LEARNING ACTIVITIES

Learning Activities

Learning *Activity 1*	Routes of Transmission
Learning *Activity* 2	Universal Precautions to Prevent HIV Transmission in Health Care settings
Learning *Activity 3*	The HIV-infected Health Care Worker
Learning *Activity* 4	Problem-solving
Learning *Activity* 5	Changing Practices in Health Care Settings

The first three Learning Activities involve the presentation of information by the instructor, followed by an examination of this information by the class by means of discussion.

Learning Activity 4 requires the students to work in groups and apply general information to very specific situations. The students then present the strategies that have been developed to the class, which then discusses them.

Learning Activity 5 is designed to prepare the student to take part in the process of developing appropriate procedures and implementing staff education.

Learning Activity 1 ROUTES OF TRANSMISSION

Present the following information and ask students to identify specific situations in which accidental contact with blood or other body fluids might occur. As they name situations, write these on the board, suggesting any others which they may have omitted, e.g., giving an injection with an unsterilized needle and syringe, assisting in the delivery of a baby without wearing gloves, having a cut on their hands, etc.

Routes of Transmission of HIV

HIV can be transmitted by exposure to infected blood or other body fluids. Body fluids which can transmit HIV include the following:

- blood
- semen
- vaginal and cervical secretions
- wound secretions
- cerebrospinal fluids
- pleural fluids
- synovial, peritoneal, pericardial and amniotic fluids

Blood is the Single most important Route of Potential Transmission of HIV Infection in health Care Settings.

Listed below are body fluids which, unless containing visible blood, have not been associated with the transmission of HIV in the health care setting. However, since some of these fluids and excretions (marked with a *) represent a potential source for nosocomial and community-acquired infections with other pathogens, nurses must exercise caution in handling them.

- faeces*
- nasal secretions*
- urine*
- sweat
- salivat*
- breastmilk*
- tears*
- vomitus*

There is a risk of HIV being transmitted in health care settings, but this risk is very small. In studies of health care workers who were exposed to HIV through needlestick injuries, the risk has been shown to be less than 0.5%. The risk of HIV transmission following mucous membrane or skin exposure to HIV-infected blood, body fluids or tissues is even lower. The risk is low but does exist.

It is sometimes suggested that all patients (and health care providers/nurses) be tested for HIV antibody as a means of protection for nurses. However, routine and/or mandatory testing of either health care workers or patients for HIV antibody is not an effective strategy for controlling HIV transmission in the health care setting and is not recommended by the World Health Organization, as it is impossible to identify all infected individuals. For example, a person may have been infected and may not yet have developed antibodies. Consequently, this person's test result will be a false negative (see *Module 2).* Therefore, even if everyone is tested for HIV antibodies, it is not possible to identify everyone who is infected. In addition, it is time-consuming and costly and may lead to a false sense of security.

After presenting the above information to the students, divide them into small groups and ask them to identify situations in clinical practice in which either health care workers or patients may be accidently exposed to HIV. Allow 30 minutes for this and then bring them back into a large group and have each group report its findings.

The instructor should list these on the board or on large sheets of paper and, following the group reports, the instructor can summarize using the information that follows.

Summary List

Bloodborne infections agents, including some Hepatitisviruses (e.g., the viruses which cause Hepatitis B and Hepatitis C) and HIV, can be transmitted in the health care setting in the following ways:

- RISK TO HEALTH CARE WORKERS:
  - Inquiry with a needle or any other sharp instrument which has been contaminated with blood o other body Raids from an HIV-infected person
  - Exposure of open wounds to blood or other body fluids from an HIV-infected person (HIV is not transmitted through unbroken skin)
  - Splashes of infected blood or body fluids onto mucous membranes and the eyes.

- RISK TO PATIENTS:
  - Contaminated instruments (needles, syringes, scalpels and other instruments for invasive procedures) that are being re-used without being adequately disinfected or sterilized
  - Transfusion with HIV-infected blood
  - Skin grab, organ transplant or donated semen from an HIV-infected donor
  - Contact with blood or other body fluids from an HIV-infected health crewelwork (e.g., midwife, surgeon, or dentist).

Finally, the instructor should reassure the students that the principal risk of HIV infection is from sexual exposure to the virus and, if appropriate infection control precautions are implemented, the transmission of HIV or any other bloodborne infectious agent is unlikely in health care settings.

Learning Activity 2 UNIVERSAL PRECAUTIONS TO PREVENT HIV TRANSMISSION IN HEALTH CARE SETTINGS

Divide the class back into small groups. Using the summary list from *Learning Activity* 1, ask the students to identify the precautions needed to prevent HIV transmission in each of the situations identified. Allow 45 minutes for this and then have each group report back to the class.

The instructor should discuss each situation comprehensively and ensure all staff recognise appropriate infection control precautions, as described below:

Infection Control Precautions

To PREVENT INJURIES FROM NEEDLES AND OTHER SHARP INSTRUMENTS:

- Never bend, break or recap disposable needles, but dispose of them immediately with the attached syringe in a thick cardboard, glass, heavy plastic or metal container. These should be located as close as is practical to the area in which the needles are used.
- Place disposable sharp instruments in a thick cardboard, glass, heavy plastic or metal container immediately after use. When full, seal the container carefully and burn or bury in a hygienically controlled sanitary landfill.
- Place re-usable sharp instruments (e.g., needles, scalpels, etc.) in a gloss, heavy plastic or metal container immediately after use. Wear thick gloves to carefully clean needles and all other sharp instruments (and syringes) before disinfection or sterilization .
- Avoid unnecessary handling of contaminated sharp instruments, including needles.

TO PREVENT EXPOSURE OF OPEN WOUNDS AND MUCOUS MEMBRANES:

- Cover broken skin or open wounds with watertight dressings.
- Wash hands with water and soap immediately after any contact with blood or other body fluids.
- Specimens of blood and other body fluids should be placed in containers with secure lids to prevent leakage during transport. Avoid contamination of the outer surface of the container.
- Wear suitable gloves when expecting exposure to blood or body fluids and when handling blood specimens.
- Linen soiled with blood and other body fluids should be transported in leak-proof bags, or folded with the soiled part inside. It should be washed in hot water with detergent.
- During assistance at childbirth, the nurse may be exposed to extensive amounts of blood. Planning for childbirth in the hospital or in the home should include obtaining gloves, aprons, soap and water.
- Wear protective glasses when blood splashes are expected, such as during major surgery, childbirth or dental procedures.
- Mouth-to-mouth suction of newborns should be replaced with mechanical or electric suction devices.
- Mouth pipetting should be replaced by mechanical pipetting in all laboratories handling blood and other body fluids.
- Resuscitation bags should be made available in health cure settings in which resuscitation is likely to be needed.

PREVENTING HIV TRANSMISSION VIA CONTAMINATED INSTRUMENTS:

- All re-usable instruments must be cleaned and disinfected or sterilized between use.
- Disposable equipment must be used only once and then appropriately discarded, i.e., burnt or buried.

- Promote oral medication rather than medication by injection when possible; if clients prefer injections, explain why oral medication is preferable.
- Teach patients to avoid injections and skin-piercing carried out by practitioners who do not sterilize their equipment.

PREVENTING HIV TRANSMISSION VIA TRANSFUSION OF HIV-CONTAMINATED BLOOD OR BLOOD PRODUCTS:

- All blood for transfusion should be tested for markers of HIV infection. In areas where testing is not feasible, blood transfusions should only be given when absolutely necessary, to treat a life-threatening condition.
- Where possible, replace blood transfusions by other suitable intravenous fluids, e.g., dextrose and/or dextran 70 or Ringer's solutions.
- For patients who are anaemic, the cause of anaemia should be sought and treated. It is better to prevent the cause of anaemia (hookworm, malaria or malnutrition) than to give transfusions.

PREVENTING HIV TRANSMISSION FROM HIV-CONTAMINATED ORGAN OR TISSUE TRANSPLANT OR SEMEN DONATION:

- Test all donors for HIV antibody prior to any donation.

SPILLS OF BLOOD OR OTHER BODY FLUIDS ONTO SURFACES (e.g. TABLE, FLOOR):

- Remove blood or other body fluids with paper towels or old newspapers. Take care not to get blood on the hands i.e. wear gloves where possible. Cloth towels may be used, but will then be contaminated and must be handled as soiled linen.
- Wash surface with hot water and soap.
- Decontaminate with intermediate or low-level disinfectant, e.g. sodium hypochlorite.

DISPOSAL OF WASTE:

- Liquid, such as blood, can be flushed into a sanitary sewer or pit latrine.
- Solid waste, for example, blood-soaked dressings, sanitary pads and napkins, placentas or tissue biopsy specimens should be burned or carefully buried. Caution: avoid placing these materials in open dumps to which animals and children have access, and avoid burying materials where there is a possibility of their being dug up or where they might contaminate water sources.

Summarize this session by reminding students that it is not possible to identify, with any degree of accuracy, who is and who is not infected with HIV. Consequently, the precautions devised to prevent HIV transmission in health care settings apply to all patients, all the time, in all clinical settings. This concept has become known as universal precautions and is now an essential feature of modern nursing practice. In addition, emphasize that the same good practice techniques will also protect patients from the remote possibility of becoming infected with HIV from an infected health care worker.

Learning Activity 3 THE HIV-INFECTED HEALTH CARE WORKER

Background Information

Only one suspected case of health care worker-to-patient transmission of HIV infection has been reported (and the route of transmission in this case has never been established}, and the chances of it occurring are very small. HIV-infected health care workers are not a risk to patients during routine work activities, but may be more so during invasive procedures. In addition, HIV infection will progressively impair the immune system and, consequently, HIV-infected health care workers are more likely to acquire nosocomial infections from patients with contagious diseases, e.g., pulmonary tuberculosis.

Divide the students into small groups and ask them to discuss the following questions:

- Should all nurses be tested for HIV antibodies?
- If a nurse knows that she/he is infected with HIV, what should she/he do?
- What restrictions should be placed on clinical assignments for health care workers known to be infected with HIV?

Allow 30 minutes for this exercise and then have each group report back to the class, to allow for open discussion. Try to arrive at some consensus of opinion and summarize important points agreed by the class.

Learning Activity 4 PROBLEM-SOLVING

Present two or three of the following situations which may commonly occur in health care settings. Read examples to the class, and have them decide whether the action taken was appropriate or inappropriate, and discuss why. This activity may also be carried out as a small group activity, in which each group discusses an individual situation and defends its decision to the class. This allows for a frank and outspoken discussion by those who may be resistant to the application of universal precautions, and is more likely to encourage better practices . Correct answers are presented to the instructor. Several possible scenarios are presented. The ones most appropriate for the students should be selected. The instructor is encouraged to develop more specific scenarios describing problems that the students may encounter in their own country.

Situations

1. A nurse arrives at a health centre to collect supplies for the outreach immunization service in a nearby village. She gets sterilized syringes, and asks .for a safe container for the used syringes. She is told to put them in a small bowl that is only large enough for the syringes and not for the needles. She says she cannot handle the needles and gets a big metal jar with a loose lid.
2. A nurse/midwife orders supplies for the following month. There is a budget, but the request is too expensive. She says, 'Well, what will it be? Gloves or a new stethoscope? My stethoscope is old, and I need gloves too. What shall I do? I will order the stethoscope!"
3. A nurse gives a patient an injection. She reminds herself not to recap a disposable needle, and looks around for a needle container. She does not see one and decides to put the cap back on the needle. (N.B. Instructors should note that disposable needles and/or syringes may not be locally available.)
4. A nurse/midwife is responsible for the training of traditional birth attendants in the district. She has ordered gloves for them, but has been told they are not available.
5. A nurse throws disposable needles in the waste container, which is emptied once a day into a plastic bag and taken to be buried.

Possible Answers

1. The nurse has found a good solution to her problem.
2. The nurse/midwife is not thinking about her personal protection. She should try very hard to have gloves always available for delivering bobbies. It is best to have a few pairs per delivery so that she can change gloves, if necessary.
3. This nurse is running a high risk! If she has no container to put the uncapped syringe in, there is another solution. Use the "scoop method", by putting the cop on the table, pushing the needle into it and, without holding the cap in the other hand, securing it.
4. If it is impossible to get gloves, the nurse/midwife should teach the traditional birth attendants to wash their hands frequently with soup and water. They should also be taught to cover any cuts they may have on their hands with waterproof dressings. N.B. Good hand-washing technique is always important!
5. The people who remove the waste are at high risk of injuring themselves from needles sticking through the plastic bog. People may collect needles. Needles need to be kept in a hard container for storage, for example, in oil cans, beer bottles or plastic bottles, until they are disposed of. (Strong cardboard boxes are better than a plastic bag!) If the needles con be burned, that is the best method of disposal. If that is not possible, they con be disposed of in a pit latrine or buried where they will not be dug up.

Learning Activity 5 CHANGING PRACTICES IN HEALTH CARE SETTINGS

Divide the class into groups and select one of the following situations for each group, or develop other situations which are appropriate for your area. Ask the group to answer the questions. Have each group appoint a recorder, who takes notes and then presents the group's plan to the class. Give a minimum of 30 minutes for the small group discussion and follow it up with 10 minutes for each group to present its respective situation and solutions.

An alternative for this activity would be to describe the situation and the solutions to the students; ask them to role-play how to teach the patient or the staff, and to write a letter to the responsible authority.

SITUATION 1

A woman brings her baby, who has a fever, to the clinic. When the baby is given tablets instead of an injection, them other becomes angry. This is a community in which nurses have given a lot of medicine by injection when available, because the people believe it works better. Sterilization procedures are difficult, given the lack of sufficient equipment needed for daily use, and the nurse is worried that clinic staff may be giving injections with unsterile equipment.

1. What are your objectives for your patient? For the community? (What do you want to accomplish?)
2. In meeting your objectives, what may be difficult to teach?
3. What could you do to convince the mother that unnecessary injections should be avoided?
4. How could you to teach others in the community that injections are not always better than pills? What information would you provide?
5. What can you do to prevent staff from using unsterile syringes and needles? What will you tell them?

Possible Answers

1. To give oral medication, when ever possible, and to avoid unnecessary injections; to try to make the mother satisfied with this; to teach staff to use sterilized needles and syringes; to obtain sufficient equipment; to teach the community about unnecessary injections.
2. Them other thinks injections are better. The community is used to injections. Hence, changing attitudes may be difficult.
3. Tell her how medicine is absorbed; draw a simple diagram to show how medicine goes into the bloodstream from the stomach.
4. Contact local community leaders and talk to them about the problem; ask their advice; request a meeting and teach groups of people what you have told the mother.
5. Plan training for the staff immediately after the clinic closes for the day. Demonstrate the correct way of handling and sterilizing

dirty syringes and needles. Provide information about how HIV is transmitted. If the problem is that there are not enough needles and syringes, obliging the clinic to re-use them, discuss with your supervisor the possibility of writing a letter to the person responsible at national level, informing him or her of your concern. Discontinue the practice of unnecessary injections. Contact a local agency, such as a church mission or the Red Cross, and ask them for more needles and syringes.

SITUATION 2

A man comes to the health centre with a fever and a swollen arm. He says he has gone to a lay practitioner for injection. The practitioner is a local leader who is highly respected in the community. You know the man would respect his advice more than yours, and are afraid he will stop coming to the clinic if you suggest that the practitioner is doing something wrong.

1. What are your objectives for the patient? For the community? (What do you want to accomplish?)
2. What problems could you face in meeting your objectives?
3. What strategies could you use to prevent the patient from seeking injections from the proctitioner?
4. What strategies could you use to teach others in the community to avoid seeking injections from lay practitioners?
5. What strategies could you use to teach local practitioners to sterilize their equipment?

Possible Answers

1. To encourage everyone in the community to avoid getting injections from untrained people; perhaps to train local practitioners.
2. The patient trusts the practitioner and the community also trusts *him. You are seen as an outsider.*
3. *Explain to the patient the mode of transmission of HIV, tetanus, and other infections. Treat the infection, which will help him gain trust in you and your expertise. Draw simple diagrams to explain about microorganisms. Find out why people go to the practitioner.*
4. Check the law to find out who is allowed to give injections. If lay practitioners cannot by low give injections or buy medicines, contact your local supervisor about the problem. Approach the practitioner and explain to them your concerns about possible HIV transmission and ask their advice. Call a meeting of local people in the community and explain to them the dangers of having injections from equipment which is not properly sterilized.
5. If the proctitioner is working within the law, explain the problem to him and offer to show how to sterilize needles and syringes. Consider ways to make more syringes available, if necessary.

SITUATION 3

Your group is a management committee in a hospital working on the development of new policies and procedures for infection control precautions to prevent the transmission of bloodborne pathogens. You are to develop a plan for teaching the staff how to use these procedures. The staff include nurses on the wards and in the emergency room, the housekeeping staff, and the laboratory workers. They have used the same procedures for twenty years, and you have already heard some laboratory staff and nurses say they want to have all patients tested for HIV antibodies.

1. What are your objectives?
2. What problems are likely to arise in meeting your objectives?
3. What changes should you make to existing policies?
4. Whom do you propose to teach about these changes?
5. How will you teach them (for example, in small or large groups, in lectures, or with demonstrations of techniques)?

Possible Answers

1. To implement universal precautions throughout the hospital and to have all staff use and understand these precautions.
2. Possible problems include: the staff are used to disease-oriented infection control precautions; they are used to other ways of doing things; they have no confidence in what you tell them; and a general shortage of supplies may exist.
3. To use precautions when dealing with blood and other body fluids from everyone; not to label specimens as infectious, but to treat them all as infectious; to wear gloves when drawing blood and during any procedure in which contact with blood or other body fluids is a possibility.
4. Everyone who may have contact with patients or specimens needs training in universal precautions. Otherwise, people will be confused when they see others changing their procedures.
5. One method would be to visit each department individually leach nursing unit, each housekeeping team, the laboratory, etc.) and provide information to small groups. Those concerned can then ask questions.

SITUATION 4

You are part of a clinical management committee that has been formed to study ways to limit the number of unnecessary blood transfusions. It has been discovered that several children may have become HIV-infected from blood transfusions. Most are anaemic as a result of malaria. You have been told that screening of blood for HIV may be set up within one year.

1. What are your objectives?
2. What are the most common medical conditions requiring blood transfusions in your work setting?
3. What other interventions are there besides blood transfusions which might solve these medical problems (both to prevent the problem and to treat the problem once it exists)?
4. Who needs to know about these solutions?
5. How will you present these solutions to them? (What kind of person will they listen to? What information will convince them that there is a problem? How can you convince them of the solutions?)

Possible Answers

1. To prevent HIV transmission by blood transfusion.

2. Malaria; sickle cell anaemia; blood loss due to haemorrhage at childbirth, trauma or surgery.
3. Malaria: identify cases early and treat the disease before the anaemia develops; discuss vector control. Sickle cell anaemia: give recommended childhood vaccines; treat all illnesses early; treat exacerbations early. Blood loss due to surgery, childbirth, trauma: check the haemoglobin content and with minor blood loss, if possible, give intravenous, high molecular fluid replacement rather than blood Strengthen antenatal services to prevent complicated labour.
4. Malaria and sickle cell anaemia: parents need to know the symptoms; nurses in district health centres need to identify cases early and to guide parents; and treatment needs to be provided. Blood loss: physicians and nurses in surgery, labour and delivery rooms and in emergency rooms.
5. Nurses can teach parents and community members. Sometimes having a meeting, and asking a respected community leader to introduce you, will give even more importance to the problem. If members of the community know that people are getting HIV infection from blood transfusions, they are more likely to be concerned. If you then present beneficial solutions, they will probably be interested in implementing them.

   In addition, nurses can become local experts on HIV infection and can arrange in-service education for their colleagues.

THE PSYCHOSOCIAL IMPACT OF HIV INFECTION ON THE INDIVIDUAL AND THE COMMUNITY

GENERAL OBJECTIVE

On completion of this module, the student should be able to identify the psychosocial factors that affect people with HIV infection, and be aware of the nurse's role in relation to social attitudes and their effects on the individual.

SPECIFIC OBJECTIVES

On completion of this module, the student should be able:

— to understand the way in which some diseases are stigmatized.

— to discuss the social and cultural attitudes and beliefs that affect individuals infected with HIV and their care.

— to describe the ways in which HIV infection might have a psychosocial impact on individuals and their community, and the relevance of social attitudes.

— to identify existing resources in the community that can meet the psychosocial needs that affected individuals can have.

— to describe the constraints that nurses work within in meeting the psychosocial needs of people with HIV (cultural, social, ethical and professional).

— to identify strategies for strengthening and developing community-based support systems for people with HIV infection.

INTRODUCTION

This module deals with the response of the community to the AIDS pandemic, the ways in which the psychosocial effects of infection are influenced by this response, and the role of nurses in decreasing these effects and strengthening community resources.

All societies affected by the AIDS pandemic have reacted with varying amounts of fear and discrimination towards those infected, or at risk of being infected with HIV. This has compounded the often devastating psychological and social consequences of an HIV diagnosis.

Nurses are, of course, members of the societies they live in and are influenced by prevailing cultural, social and religious attitudes. This can sometimes affect their attitudes towards those they care for and lead to conflicts with professional guidelines. Nurses who are working to change social attitudes about any aspect of AIDS care or prevention can find themselves at odds with their communities and with local policies relating to HIV. Nurses in many countries have developed proven strategies to tackle these difficulties, but always have to work within certain constraints.

LEARNING ACTIVITIES

LEARNING ACTIVITIES KEY (MODULE 4)

Learning Activity 1	Stigma and Disease
Learning Activity 2	Attitudes to HIV and AIDS
Learning Activity 3	Psychosocial Impact of HIV Infection on the individual
Learning Activity 4	A Personal Experience with HIV Infection
Learning Activity 5	Existing Resources for Support in the Community
Learning Activity 6	Constraints and Strategies for Nurses

Ground Rules

Whenever people discuss personal attitudes and beliefs about controversial subjects, there is the possibility that strong feelings might be expressed. AIDS raises issues connected with sexuality, death, drug use, prejudices, morals, religion and many other difficult areas. For this reason, it is important that students feel safe enough to discuss such issues. Therefore, before beginning any of the Learning Activities, it is worth spending 15 minutes establishing some rules that will provide a framework that encourages participation.

One way of doing this is for the teacher to stand beside a large sheet of paper or writing board and write up a set of agreed ground rules that will be displayed throughout the module. The teacher and the student group are jointly responsible for ensuring that the rules are observed.

The teacher can begin this process by asking the students what would make it easier for them to discuss their attitudes and beliefs about AIDS and the related social issues. Each suggestion should be discussed and agreed upon before being added to the list of ground rules.

If the group has difficulty in deciding its own rules the teacher may make suggestions. Here are some possible ground rules that have been found to facilitate group discussion:

— no pressure on students to share personal views and experiences
— confidentiality to apply to any information that is shared
— respecting the rights of others to hold opinions we disagree with
— making sure everyone has the opportunity to speak.

The establishing of such ground rules should create suitable conditions for proceeding with the Learning Activities, but it is possible that further adjustments to the rules may be necessary.

Learning Activity 1 STIGMA AND DISEASE

Tell the students that they are going to compare social attitudes and beliefs about AIDS with those held about other diseases.

Divide the class into discussion groups of 3 to 5 members. Ask each group to elect a leader who can record the group's ideas and report them back to the class. Each group will need a pen and a (preferably large) sheet of paper.

Ask each small group to call out, in turn, the name of a disease that affects people in their community. Ensure that there is as little duplication as possible. Ask each leader to divide their sheet of paper into two columns. They should then write "AIDS" at the head of one column and the other disease they named at the head of the other.

Tell the groups that they have 15 minutes to list as many ways as possible in which AIDS and the other disease are seen as being different by members of their community. Inform the students that these differences may be the result of differences in attitudes, beliefs, theories, religious ideas and so on.

When the task has been completed, ask each of the group leaders to present to the class a summary of the differences identified by the groups.

Then invite the whole class to discuss the reasons why they think AIDS is seen as being different from many other diseases, and what implications this might have for individuals with AIDS.

Summarize the key points that emerged during the Learning Activity.

Learning Activity 2 ATTITUDES TO HIV AND AIDS

Tell the students that in this session they will have the opportunity to explore and clarify their own attitudes towards HIV and AIDS. Invite them to be as honest as possible, and remind them of the ground rules they agreed.

Divide the class into smaller discussion groups of 3 to 5 members. Ask each group to elect a leader who can record the group's ideas and report them back to the class. Each group member will need a copy of the statements listed below. Alternatively the statements can be written up and displayed for all the students to see.

Here is the list of statements that can be used. Other statements may be added or substituted as the teacher wishes.

Statements

1. People with AIDS are to blame for bringing this disease on themselves.
2. Nurses should be able to refuse to care for a patient with AIDS.
3. The AIDS epidemic could be stopped if laws against prostitution and homosexual behaviour were made stronger, and if foreigners were sent home.
4. People with AIDS should have the same rights as all other patients.
5. HIV is a just punishment for immoral behaviour.
6. All nurses should be tested for HIV antibodies and removed from practice if found to be positive.
7. Nurses should have no fears at all about caring for people with AIDS.
8. All patients should be tested for HIV antibodies, whether they consent to it or not.
9. People with HIV who continue to have sex should be put in prison.
10. People in my community will never use condoms to protect themselves against HIV because they encourage immoral behaviour.

First of all, ask the students as individuals to write their own individual responses to each of the statements provided. Encourage them not simply to put "yes" or "no", "agree" or "disagree", but to give reasons in support of their views. After approximately 10 minutes ask them to discuss their responses in their small groups. Their goal is to agree on a group answer that reflects the views of the individual students involved. Obviously this stage involves a considerable amount of debate so allow longer, maybe 20 to 30 minutes.

Then, with the class, deal with each of the statements in turn, asking some or all of the small group leaders to report on the ideas expressed in their groups.

It is important that the teacher does not seek to correct or criticize views that he or she disagrees with at this stage, but allows a free expression of them. The teacher should facilitate any discussion that ensues for the remainder of the time allocated for this Learning Activity.

Learning Activity 3 PSYCHOSOCIAL IMPACT OF HIV INFECTION ON THE INDIVIDUAL

This Learning Activity is intended to increase students' understanding of the psychosocial consequences of HIV infection and how these can be influenced by social attitudes.

First of all, ask the students to work individually on a written task. This task could be set as homework before the start of the session to save time.

The students should be asked to imagine themselves in the position of someone who has just found out that they are HIV-infected, and to write a list of what they think their likely needs would be:

— in the first 24 hours following the diagnosis
— in the first two weeks
— in the first six months.

Remind the students that these needs may be physical, psychological, social or spiritual.

Get the students to work in small groups of 3 to 5 with elected leaders. Ask them to share their written work with each other, and to produce a list of the seven most important needs at each of the three stages following diagnosis (there will probably be some needs that get listed in each of the "stages").

The teacher should then ask one of the group leaders to present the findings of their particular group, preferably writing the "needs" in three columns, corresponding to the three periods listed above, on a board at the front of the class. The other group leaders can be asked if they have anything to add that is not already covered.

Once this process has been completed, the teacher will be able to make some summarizing comments:

1. Although nurses commonly focus on the physical aspects of; HIV infection this exercise usually reveals that a majority of the needs expressed are psychological or social in nature. This underlines the importance of good psycholocial care.
2. The lists of needs produced by the groups are usually very similar. The students can be assured that if the same task were carried out by a group of HIV-positive people, the resulting lists would also be similar. This helps them to see that a) peple with HIV are not so different from themselves, that b) they have an ability to be empathic, and that c) there is a lot of scope for effective nursing interventions to meet the large number of psychosocial needs.

In the second stage of this Learning Activity the teacher takes each of the "needs" listed in front of the class and asks the students to supply for each different one:

- — one way in which the community response (attitudes or behaviour) to that infected individual might be unhelpful, or make matters worse
- — one way in which a nurse might be helpful in meeting that need.

This further work can be carried out in front of the whole class with the teacher in a facilitating role, or may be done, once again, in small groups and then fed back to the class by the leaders of the smaller groups.

Learning Activity 4 A PERSONAL EXPERIENCE OF HIV INFECTION

For this activity, a person with HIV or AIDS is invited to speak to the class. It is often the case, particularly in areas of low seroprevalence, that face-to-face contact of this kind is the most effective way of encouraging nurses to empathize with affected people. Specifically, they become more aware of the personal impact of the disease and more able to gauge the likely effects of their own attitudes, and those of the community, upon people with HIV infection or HIV-related illnesses.

Typically such a session would begin with the person with HIV or AIDS telling the group something of their personal story. Then the students can be invited to ask questions. This structure should be varied to suit the wishes of the visiting speaker.

It is very important that the invited person should feel comfortable talking to groups of students and should be prepared by the teacher for the types of questions that may be asked. It is essential that the teacher spends some time with the guest speaker after the session to discuss how it went and listen to any points the speaker wishes to raise.

It is also possible that the students might feel uncomfortable asking questions, in case their classmates think they are being rude or showing their ignorance. One way of encouraging free communication is to ask the students to prepare their questions in advance by writing them on small pieces of paper, anonymously. The teacher can then collect them in and ask a selection of questions. Another advantage of this method is that inappropriate questions can be screened out!

At the end of the session, while the teacher is talking it over with the guest speaker, the students can be asked to discuss their reactions in small groups. A large group discussion can then be held when the teacher returns for the remaining time available.

Learning Activity 5 EXISTING RESOURCES FOR SUPPORT IN THE COMMUNITY

In this session, existing resources will be identified and linked to the meeting of specific needs.

The list of needs compiled in *Learning Activity 3* should be used as the basis for this session. The list of needs should be reviewed in the light of the personal experience of the person with HIV/AIDS, who came to speak to the students during *Learning Activity 4,* before proceeding. It is also important that the teacher has a good level of knowledge about possible sources of support for people with HIV/AIDS.

Ask the group to take each "need" in turn and list all the community resources that might be utilized. These might include professionals, AIDS-specific community organizations, other community organizations, informal and family relationships, statutory and religious bodies.

This exercise is probably best done in the large group setting. The students will be better able to pool their knowledge, the teacher will be able to fill in gaps, and unnecessary duplication can be avoided.

Once a comprehensive list has been compiled the students could do some project work in small groups; if time allows they could undertake to visit or write to some of the individuals or organizations mentioned and then report back to their fellow students. This is an effective way of increasing the knowledge of the whole group about the resources available.

Learning Activity 6 CONSTRAINTS AND STRATEGIES FOR NURSES

This session allows nurses to acknowledge and explore the factors that limit them to some extent from meeting the perceived needs of people with HIV and AIDS, and to develop possible strategies to minimize these limitations. It is important that difficulties can be faced honestly but it is also important that the nurses can experience being potentially effective agents of change.

For this learning activity the students must have access to the International Council of Nurses Code for Nurses and any national, local or hospital policies relating to HIV/AIDS (if such policies exist). It will be helpful if these materials have been read by some or all of the students before beginning the learning activity. If this is impractical, the materials should at least be on hand for reference.

Divide the students into small groups of 3 to 5 with elected leaders who can report back to the large group.

Ask the group to reflect on their experiences of *Module 4* as a whole and to spend 20 minutes answering the following questions.

The questions should be put up on a board at the front of the class or copies supplied to each group.

QUESTIONS:

1. What barriers and limitations might nurses face in your community in trying to meet the needs of people with HIV/AIDS?
2. Are there any conflicts between the International Code for Nurses, any local policies that you are aware of, and actual nursing practice that you have seen?
3. Why do you think these inconsistencies exist?
4. Can anything be done to tackle these inconsistencies?

The group leaders should write down the group responses. Some or all of the group leaders should then be invited to report back, and the teacher can then facilitate a discussion in the class about the various points raised.

DEVELOPING COUNSELLING SKILLS

GENERAL OBJECTIVE

On completion of this module, the student should be able to understand the basic theory and practice of counselling as it relates to people with HIV/AIDS and to preventing the spread of HIV. They should feel able to begin using the skills themselves with adequate guidance and support.

SPECIFIC OBJECTIVES

On completion of this module the student should be able:

- to identify the counselling skills that are appropriate when talking to patients in the context of HIV
- to understand why counselling skills are important in relation to HIV
- to be aware of the barriers that obstruct effective communication
- to reflect on examples from their own clinical practice where counselling skills could have been used more effectively
- to understand the issues involved in pre- and post-HIV antibody test counselling.

INTRODUCTION

Counselling in the field of HIV/AIDS is sometimes provided by specialist counsellors who have been trained for that specific role.

More often, however, other health and social care professionals use counselling skills in the course of their work to achieve similar goals. However, all health and social care professionals use communication skills that are the foundations of such counselling skills.

Levels of Expertise

Communication skills: Listening and advising as part of carer's professional role.
Counselling skills: Focusing on fears and specific problems; helping individuals to formulate strategies and coping mechanisms.
Counselling: Formal use of a counselling model within a designated professional relationship, to alleviate psychological distress.

In the field of HIV/AIDS, counselling skills can be used in any encounter between nurses and patients. In practice they are used in two basic ways:

1. Preventing transmission of HIV infection
2. Providing psychosocial support to those infected or affected (e.g., a patient's family) by HIV.

A diagnosis of HIV infection or AIDS, or even discussion of the possibility of infection, is stressful. People have to face the possibility of many changes, losses and adjustments, often in situations of social isolation or poverty. There will be implications for all aspects of their lives. Patients can be overwhelmed by the number of problems and potential problems that they face. There is some evidence that life expectancy can actually be shorter in patients who feel least supported. There is a good deal of evidence that quality of life can be improved by appropriate counselling interventions.

These patients can be greatly helped if they can talk about their problems . At the very least, two minds are better than one at sorting out alternatives and fully exploring the issues involved.

Also, any discussions about HIV will be more effective if counselling skills are used to explore specific issues for individuals. It is tempting for busy health professionals simply to give information and advice and then leave the patient to fend for themselves. This approach can only be of limited effectiveness. Information given within a supportive framework is more likely to be acted upon. Just as health professionals can lapse into impersonal "advice giving", patients sometimes appear to want their carers to adopt this role. It is natural, in the short term, for distressed people to want carers to "take over" and do their thinking for them. However, patients who are told what to do take longer to find the answers most suited to their own personalities and circumstances.

Counselling skills, properly used, are simply tools to help individuals seek and final their own solutions to the dilemmas they face.

LEARNING ACTIVITIES

LEARNING ACTIVITIES KEY (MODULE 5)

Learning Activity 1 Rationale for the Use of Counselling Skills in HIV/AIDS
Learning Activity 2 Barriers to Effective Communication
Learning Activity 3 Reflections on Clinical Practice
Learning Activity 4 Issues in Pre- and Post-Test Counselling

Learning Activity 1 RATIONALE FOR THE USE OF COUNSELLING SKILLS IN HIV/AIDS

The students should be given the opportunity to revise any previous learning about basic communication and counselling skills before this session. However, even if they have done very little learning about this topic in the past, this learning activity can still be useful .

After introducing the topic, tell the students that they are going to be exploring the qualities that are needed for the effective application of counselling skills.

Divide the class into two groups. If possible, arrange for one of the groups to work in another room.. Say that you would like one group to take the viewpoint of two types of patient:

— type a) a patient seeking advice on HIV prevention
— type b) a recently diagnosed HIV-infected patient.

Give this group a large sheet of paper and the opportunity to elect a leader who will write down their ideas and present them later. Then ask the students in this group to spend 20 minutes listing all the personal qualities that they would want from a nurse in both cases. How would they want the nurse to behave towards them? What kind of skills would they want to see if they were going to find an encounter with the nurse beneficial?

Equip the other group with a sheet of paper too, and give them the opportunity to elect a leader. Ask them to spend 20 minutes listing all the personal qualities and interpersonal skills that might help them to be effective in terms of:

— prevention
— support.

Then ask the two leaders to swap groups. The "patient" leader will go into the "nurse" group and the "nurse" leader will go into the "patient" group.

Ask the two leaders to brief to the group they have moved to and to discuss any issues that arise. Do the "nurses" and "patients" feel that the needs and skills explored are compatible? The teacher should move between the two groups to observe what is going on. This stage should take a further 20 minutes.

At the end of this time the two groups should join together again and spend another 20 minutes in a teacher-led discussion about what has been learned in the exercise and what the implications are for nursing practice.

Learning Activity 2 BARRIERS TO EFFECTIVE COMMUNICATION

Counselling skills are specialized forms of communication skills. Nurses spend almost all their time communicating with patients. Verbal and non-verbal messages that pass between nurse and patient can have therapeutic or non-therapeutic qualities and outcomes .

In HIV/AIDS the combination of patients with complex needs, together with the demands of busy nursing staff, can produce a less than therapeutic environment where communication is blocked by various barriers. In this Learning Activity, the students will be able to increase their level of awareness of these barriers.

Begin by telling the students that they will be doing an exercise about communication. Divide them into pairs and ask them to decide between themselves who is partner I and who is partner 2. Then say that for the next 5 minutes you want all the "1" s to talk to their "2"s about a pleasant personal experience (you can suggest topics like: a favourite meal, a long journey, a favourite film, etc.). Tell the listener in each pair that their role is to listen attentively and not to interrupt. After the teacher has let the 1's speak for 5 minutes, stop them and ask them to swap roles with the 2' s, who must also select a similar topic and speak about it for 5 minutes.

Then request that the students reflect back on the exercise and ask:

a) if they were aware of any barriers or difficulties that affected their ability to communicate when it was their turn to be the speaker
b) if they could think of anything that would have helped them to communicate more freely
c) how they would have felt discussing something of a deeply personal or distressing nature instead of a pleasant experience.

The teacher should then discuss with the class what they feel they have learned from the experience and what are the implications for their nursing practice.

Learning Activity 3 REFLECTION ON CLINICAL PRACTICE

Counselling skills are difficult to learn in the classroom setting.

A nurse's counselling skills tend to improve with practice in the clinical setting. This improvement is helped by having the opportunity to reflect on their practices. Increasingly the value of such a process is being recognized in the caring professions. The opportunity to reflect on practice can be very helpful, both as a learning tool and as something that has a direct impact on the quality of nursing care.

This Learning Activity can be adapted to suit any client load, as it is not AIDS-specific. When these modules are being used by students with little experience of HIV/AIDS, other clinical experience can be the subject of reflection. The process is the same.

Tell the students that they are going to be working in small groups of 3 to 5 members for the next 50 minutes. They will not be feeding back any information to the class about their discussions so it is not necessary to elect group leaders. The discussions that take place in the groups are to be confidential, and information shared in them should not be passed on.

Each group should have a list of the questions on the next page, or be able to see them displayed at the front of the class.

Tell the students that once they are settled in their groups they should each think of an incident with a patient that has left them troubled in some way; either because they feel they did not handle the situation well or because they were left with difficult feelings afterwards. Suggest that the students take it in turns to reflect on these incidents using the framework of questions above as a guide. Encourage the group members to be supportive and understanding of one another.

The class should be re-convened by the teacher for the final 10 minutes and asked how it felt to do the exercise. It would not be appropriate to ask for details about what went on in the various groups.

- How would you describe the incident in detail?
- How did the incident make you feel at the time?
- What do you feel about it now?
- How do you feel about anyone else who was involved?
- Is there anything that you or another professional could have done more effectively in the circumstances?
- What might have helped in the situation?
- Which counselling skills might have been helpful in the incident and how might they have affected the outcome?
- Is there anything that you would still like to do in relation to the incident?
- How would you feel about facing a similar incident in the future?

Learning Activity 4 ISSUES IN PRE-TEST AND POST-TEST COUNSELLING

Many nurses become involved in counselling related to the HIV antibody test. Sometimes they have had little training, and sometimes the amount of counselling that takes place is minimal. Different societies have various practices in relation to testing. For example, if an individual has little or no choice about whether or not they are tested, pre-test counselling may be undervalued if it is seen purely as a means of obtaining informed consent to testing.

It could be argued that some kind of psychological preparation for the test and its possible implications is still important even where freedom of choice is limited. Therefore, whatever the current practices are in a particular community in relation to testing, most of the issues raised for the individual being tested are similar to those anywhere. As has been mentioned earlier in this module, counselling skills are best learned by experience. In the classroom role-play is a technique that can be used to "rehearse" possible interventions at a safe distance from real patients. Even when there is little likelihood that a particular group of students is going to be involved in this kind of counselling in the clinical area, role-play can be a useful way of bringing the issues involved to life.

Nevertheless, role-play is not always popular with teachers or students. Some find it too difficult, embarrassing or unreal. If the teacher is not confident using the technique, it is best avoided, otherwise role-play may become still more unpopular!

An alternative approach which is almost as effective, and which can be more acceptable to students, is a structured discussion. Instead of playing the roles of, for example, a nurse in a testing centre and a client seeking counselling prior to a test, two students could pair up and discuss the issues involved from the viewpoints of the nurse and the patient respectively. The exercise could also be done in threes, with the third member acting as a neutral presence. After allowing the discussion to continue for 10 minutes they could stop and talk about the various issues raised for a further 10 minutes before returning to the class for a teacher-led discussion in which they can pool their ideas. The same exercise could be repeated in relation to post-test counselling.

If, however, the role-play method is to be used, here are some suggestions:

Pre-test Counselling

The WHO guidelines (Chapter-13) could be set as a reading assignment to be completed before the session. Alternatively the teacher could present the material.

Reassure the students that they will not be role-playing in front of the whole class but will be working in threes: nurse/counsellor, patient, and observer. If there are students left over they can become extra observers.

Do not force the group to use role-play if they do not want to, but explore what it is they do not like about it, before reverting to the structured discussion method.

Tell the students who are playing the "patient" role not to invent stories or personalities that are too extreme or difficult to deal with. Suggest that they maintain their own personalities but with a few minor modifications and some plausible fictitious reason why they might have come for a test. They should also not behave as if they have a lot of information about HIV.

Do not let the role-play run for more than 10 minutes.

The observers should watch the interaction in their groups carefully and give feedback for ten minutes following the role-play.

The nurse/counsellor should imagine that they are working in a testing centre. They should use counselling skills to help the patient come to a decision about whether to have the test. Reassure them that much more time than 10 minutes would be needed for this process!

Once the role-play and the ensuing debriefing in threes has been completed, re-assemble the class and spend 10 minutes asking what the students have learned from the experience.

Post-test Counselling

Prepare a number of small pieces of paper (folded up) bearing the words "Your patient is HIV-antibody positive"; one for each group of three.

Ask the students to return to their roles and give the "results" to the nurse/counsellors.

Tell them that they have a further 10 minutes to work in their threes followed by 10 minutes debriefing time.

Once again re-assemble them in the class and ask them what they have learned from the experience.

If time permits, they might want to use the same method but have an opportunity to change roles. Also, they might want to use the same technique to role-play a discussion on HIV prevention between a nurse and a patient.

PATIENT EDUCATION

GENERAL OBJECTIVE

On completion of this module, the student will, in culturally appropriate terms, be able to describe to a person the measures he or she can take to prevent infection with HIV.

SPECIFIC OBJECTIVES

On completion of this module the student should be able:

- to describe patterns of sexual behaviour in their community
- to identify personal feelings, cultural and religious values and taboos which might affect the nurse' s ability to educate patients about HIV transmission and its prevention
- to describe in culturally acceptable terms how drug and alcohol use may be related to HIV infection and how to reduce the risk
- to discuss risk reduction with patients in the health care setting.

INTRODUCTION

Nurses are well placed to provide education aimed at reducing the risk of HIV transmission. They are perceived as reliable sources of health information and people often feel more comfortable discussing personal matters with them than with others. People' s sexual and drug-using behaviour is normally a very private matter, so nurses need to be skilled at putting people at their ease when discussing potentially embarrassing topics.

Counselling skills are needed to enable patients to make viable and sensible health choices so that they can protect themselves and others. It is essential that nurses are able to convey detailed and accurate information about sexual and drug-using behaviour in a culturally appropriate way. The transmission of HIV is preventable. It is therefore vital that there is no misunderstanding about exactly how the virus is, and is not, transmitted.

LEARNING ACTIVITIES

LEARNING ACTIVITIES KEY (MODULE 6)

Learning Activity 1	Patterns of Sexual Behaviour
Learning Activity 2	Barriers to Health Education
Learning Activity 3	Relative Risks in Sexual Behaviours
Learning Activity 4	Discussing Risk Reduction
Learning Activity 5	Discussing Substance Use
Learning Activity 6	Risk Reduction in Substance Use

GROUND RULES

Whenever people discuss personal attitudes and beliefs about controversial subjects, there is the possibility that strong feelings might be expressed. AIDS raises issues connected with sexuality, death, drug use, prejudice and many other difficult areas. For this reason it is important that students feel safe enough to discuss such issues. Therefore, before beginning any of the Learning Activities, it is worth spending 15 minutes establishing some rules, as suggested previously, that will provide a framework that encourages participation.

One way of doing this is for the teacher to stand beside a large sheet of paper or writing board and write up a set of agreed ground rules that will be displayed throughout the module. The teacher and student group are jointly responsible for ensuring that the rules are observed.

The teacher can begin this process by asking the students what would make it easier for them to discuss their attitudes and beliefs about AIDS and the related social issues. Each suggestion should be discussed and agreed upon before being added to the list of ground rules.

If the group has difficulty in deciding on its own rules the teacher may make suggestions. Here are some possible ground rules that have been found to facilitate group discussion:

— no pressure on students to share personal views and experiences

— confidentiality to apply to any information that is shared

— respecting the rights of other to hold opinions we disagree with
— making sure everyone has the opportunity to speak.

Learning Activity 1 PATTERNS OF SEXUAL BEHAVIOUR

Explain to the group that because HIV is mainly sexually transmitted, it is important that they are aware of patterns of sexual activity in their community. Reassure them that although it can sometimes be uncomfortable for them to discuss sexual issues, they will be doing a lot of the work in small groups and will be under no pressure to reveal any personal information.

Ask the students to pair up with someone in the group that they normally feel comfortable talking with and with whom they would feel least embarrassed discussing sexual matters. Assure them that they will not have to feed any information back to the class unless they wish to.

Then ask them (in their pairs) to discuss the following questions - which should be displayed for them at the front of the class. One member of each pair should write down their answers, but the written work will not be collected in by the teacher. This should be made clear.

About 30 minutes should be allowed for this part of the Learning Activity.

QUESTIONS

In our community, in your opinion:

- What are the cultural, religious and social norms (or "rules") that influence sexual behaviour? Do you agree with them or not?
- In what ways do these norms help to prevent the spread of HIV?
- Are there any ways in which these norms encourage the spread of HIV?
- By whom and in what ways are these norms not always followed?
- Why do you think that people sometimes fail to follow these norms of behaviour?
- Are there differences in what is socially acceptable for men and for women in terms of sexual behaviour?
- In what do you think sexual behaviour has changed since the start of the AIDS pandemic?

Next ask each pair to join up with another pair in the room. Any "left over" pair can be asked to join any of the groups of four. Tell them that they have a further 20 minutes to share and discuss their answers in their small groups.

When that stage has been completed ask them all to return to the class.

For the final 10 minutes the teacher can either:

a) Discuss how the group felt about doing the exercise; or
b) Ask the group for concluding statements about the main ways in their community that patterns of sexual behaviour are related to the spread of HIV infection.

If they have found the exercise embarrassing or difficult, the first alternative would be the best choice. The group may need extra time in addressing their difficulties in discussing sexual matters if they are going to continue with the module. It is very important that such difficulties are not seen as failures by the teacher. Indeed there is a positive aspect to such difficulties because they are similar to those that their patients might have in discussing sexual matters. Confronting their own difficulties will help the students to empathize with their patients and be sensitive to their problems.

If, on the other hand, the group has been able to discuss these questions with little difficulty, alternative b will further enhance their confidence during discussions of sexual matters in the larger group.

Learning Activity 2 BARRIERS TO HEALTH EDUCATION

This Learning Activity is intended to make the students more aware of the obstacles they face in becoming more effective health educators. They will also be able to identify strategies that enable them to tackle some of the obstacles they face, and will hopefully begin to perceive themselves as agents of social change.

Tell the students that in the session they will be able to discuss the problems they face in becoming more effective as health educators, as well as think about some ways of dealing with these problems.

Divide them up into small groups of 3 to 5 members with an elected leader who will record the proceedings of the group and report information back to the class.

Each group should be given a large sheet of paper and a pen and asked to divide the paper into four quarters with the following headings:

Personal	Professional
Interpersonal/Social	Religious/Cultural

Now give them approximately 20 minutes in which to list the various barriers or difficulties they face in becoming more effective health educators, under each of the headings.

When they have completed their lists, ask some or all of the group leaders to report back to the class.

Now ask the small groups to go through their lists again circling the items that they feel unable to do anything about (e.g., under the "Religious/Cultural" heading there may be items like, "It is not acceptable for a female nurse to discuss sexual matters with a male patient").

Then on a second large sheet of paper, ask the small groups to

a) draw up a realistic plan of action that would help them to deal with the problems that they have not circled and
b) list the ways in which they think their community would need to change in order to reduce the circled problems.

Again allow approximately 20 minutes for this stage. After the group leaders have again reported back, facilitate a large group discussion of the issues raised and the different ideas put forward.

Learning Activity 3 RELATIVE RISKS IN SEXUAL BEHAVIOURS

The teacher should tell the class that in this session they will be learning about the risks involved in different types of sexual behaviour, and will become more familiar with using culturally appropriate sexual language. If the group is feeling fairly confident by now about discussing sexual matters, the session can be done as a teacher-led, large-group activity. If the students are still uncomfortable in this area, they will find it easier to work in small groups, with the teacher giving the correct answers to the class afterwards.

Begin by explaining that all human activities have risks attached to them but that there are ways of minimizing these risks. A light-hearted way of beginning the session is to ask the groups how many (non-sexual) ways they have risked their lives in order to be in class today. Write them on the board and then ask them to think of ways in which they minimize the risks attached to these daily activities. Explain that, in principle, sexual behaviour is similar to the behaviours they have discussed, and that there are relatively safe and relatively unsafe forms of sexual behaviour in terms of HIV transmission.

If this Learning Activity is being undertaken in the class, you should at this point stick two signs on the wall, some distance apart. One sign should say "MOST DANGEROUS" and the other one should say "MOST SAFE". You must also have prepared in advance a large number of cards or strips of paper. Each card should bear the name of one particular behaviour and sometimes a few words of explanation for the less familiar activities. The sexual behaviours should be considered as taking place with an HIV-infected partner.

LIST OF SEXUAL BEHAVIOURS

Sexual fantasy
Masturbation (touching ones own genitals in a way that feels good sexually)

Mutual Masturbation (Two people touching each other's genitals)
Kissing on the cheek
Kissing mouth to mouth
Hugging
Vaginal intercourse without a condom
Vaginal intercourse with a properly used condom
Anal intercourse (penis in the anus) without a condom
Anal intercourse (penis in the anus) with a properly used condom
Cunnilingus (mouth contact with a woman's genitals)
Fellatio without a condom (mouth contact with a man's genitals)
Fellatio with a condom (mouth contact with a man's genitals)

Hand out the cards at random to members of the group and ask them in turn to pin or stick their card on the wall at a point between the two signs at which they feel it belongs. If they are not able even to guess where their card should go, they can pass their card on to someone else. If no-one in the group is prepared to have a guess, the teacher should pin it up. Each person who goes up to the wall with a card relating to a sexual behaviour can ask the group if they know of any words used in their community to describe the behaviour on the card. Also, each person who goes up to the wall can say whether they disagree with the positions of any cards that are already there.

Finally the teacher should move any cards that are clearly in the wrong place. The following information should be of use in doing so.

RISK-ASSOCIATED SEXUAL BEHAVIOURS

Anal intercourse without a condom should be the most dangerous of the behaviours displayed, closely followed by vaginal intercourse without a condom. There is evidence that anal intercourse is a more efficient way of transmitting the virus. As with vaginal intercourse, the receiving partner is most at risk.

Anal intercourse with a condom, followed by vaginal intercourse with a condom should probably be next. There is evidence that condoms are more easily damaged or slip off during anal intercourse.

There should then be a large gap with all the other behaviours clustered at the "Safer" end of the continuum. Cunnilingus and fellatio without a condom can justifiably be considered to be the most risky items in this group, even though evidence would suggest that the level of risk is very low. It should be emphasized that any risk involved might be increased if the oral mucosa is not intact for any reason. Also, other STD's can be transmitted in this way more easily than HIV. Mouth to mouth kissing has not been implicated in the transmission of HIV.

This exercise can be scaled down for work in small groups, if desired. Instead of the two signs they can have two headings at either end of a large sheet of paper. They can then discuss where the various behaviours (listed on a board at the front of the class) should be written down on the continuum to best represent the degree of risk involved.

Learning Activity 4 DISCUSSING RISK REDUCTION

For this Learning Activity the students need to have access to information on safe condom use. If locally available materials are inadequate or difficult to obtain the following guidelines can be reproduced. It will be helpful if the teacher demonstrates the stages involved in safe condom use, using either an anatomical model, an appropriate object or the fingers of a volunteer from the class. This last option often causes much amusement which can help to "break the ice" in the activities that follow the demonstration.

SAFE CONDOM USE

- Always use a new condom. Condoms should only be used once.
- Store condoms in a safe place where they cannot be damaged by heat or moisture.
- When taking the condom out of its wrapper, be careful not to damage it.
- The condom can only be put onto an erect penis and should be put on before there is any penetration.
- Before putting the condom on, squeeze the first centimetre of the closed end to remove trapped air which would place a strain on the condom during intercourse.
- Hold the condom over the tip of the penis and unroll it carefully as far as it will go. If the condom is the wrong way round it will not unroll. If this happens the condom should be discarded and another one used. Ensure that the partner is relaxed and sufficiently around for penetration to be comfortable. Forced or dry sex is a common cause of condom breakage.
- If additional lubrication is needed it should never be oil-based or greasy because that weakens the rubber of the condom.
- After climax the base of the condom should be gripped firmly and the penis should be withdrawn.
- Dispose of the used condom safely.

Begin the Learning Activity by telling the students that discussions with patients about sexual risk reduction are not simply a matter of relaying information about HIV transmission and safe condom use. Sexual behaviour always takes place in a context, and there are many factors that influence people's ability to make safer choices in terms of sexual behaviour. Effective communication skills are essential in any discussion of sexual behaviour with a patient, because they need to discuss the information in relation to their own life circumstances and problems.

Explain that they are going to be given a series of case studies and asked to describe the advice and information that they would give to the individuals involved, together with any counselling needs that are likely to emerge in each of the cases.

Alternatively, if the group is familiar and comfortable with role-play as an educational method, they could be asked to work in threes (nurse, patient and observer) taking it in turns to pretend to be one of the individuals in the case studies. They could choose an imaginary setting of a community clinic, or another that they are more familiar with.

Whichever of these two methods is used, the teacher should encourage the students to avoid giving moralistic answers but to work from a view point that the "patient" can make sense of in terms of their own life circumstances. It should also be pointed out that it will not always be possible for people to change their behaviour - whatever the consequences - and that this is not the fault of the health educator.

Divide the students up into small groups of 3 to 5 members with an elected leader who can take notes about the group process and report to the class, if called upon to do so.

Each group should receive a copy of the following case histories for discussion. About 30 minutes should be allowed for this stage of the activity.

CASE HISTORIES

1. Mr. A. has been treated several times for various sexually transmuted diseases and enjoys having many female sex partners. He says that he enjoys his lifestyle too much to change it but recently has begun to worry about HIV.
2. Mrs. B. has been married for several years. Her husband travels a lot and is away for weeks at a time. She fears that he may be having sex with other women, and worries that this might lead to her getting HIV. She is afraid to discuss the subject with him in case he becomes angry. He wants more children but she does not.
3. Mr. C. is 15 years old and has a girlfriend. He has had some sexual experience, but is very ignorant about how HIV is spread and how condoms are used. He asks for detailed information.
4. Mrs. D. sells sexual services to support her family. She says that condoms are expensive and that her clients offer her more money if she does not use them.
5. Mr. E. and his girlfriend have been having sex for three months. Usually they use condoms. If no condom is available they have other forms of safer sex. He wants to know when they can stop having to take these precautions, since one day they would like to have children.
6. Mr. F. is bisexual (has sex with men and women) and says that he does not enjoy sex as much when he uses condoms. He feels embarrassed about using them, and is afraid his partners will suspect he is HIV-positive if he suggests their use. He does not know whether he has HIV or not.

Learning Activity 5 DISCUSSING SUBSTANCE USE

SUBSTANCE USE AND HIV TRANSMISSION

There are many substances which people might use to alter their moods and perceptions. Societies and cultures hold different beliefs about these substances; what may be acceptable to some will be unacceptable, or even illegal, to others. A particular substance may be seen as a socially acceptable medicine or as a dangerous and illegal drug.

Whatever beliefs people have about the use of such substances and about the people who use them, it is important to have an understanding of the potential link between some substance use and the spread of HIV.

The pattern of substance use in any society con have an influence on HIV transmission in two ways:

— because of practices connected with the administration of the substance

— because of the effect the substance can have on perception, judgement and behaviour.

By understanding the background against which substance use occurs, the nurse may be able to make effective health education interventions that reduce the risk of HIV transmission .

This Learning Activity is intended to make students aware of the different types of substances that may be used. Students will also be able to discuss cultural attitudes and beliefs that surround substance use.

Divide the students up into groups of 4 to 8, with an elected leader who will write down on paper the answers and report to the class.

Each group is given a set of cards which have names of substances on them, e.g., opium, cocaine, tobacco, alcohol etc., plus a pen and a large sheet of paper with the following headings:

—	*Depressants*	—	*Hallucinogens*
—	Stimulants	—	Opiates

Each group is then asked to list the substance names given on the cards under the appropriate heading and give their reasons for doing so. Give the group 10 minutes in which to accomplish this task. When they have completed this exercise, ask the group leaders to report back to the class.

During the feedback from the group leaders, the teacher facilitates discussion on substances that have been put into the various categories and mistakes are rectified. The teacher writes or has prepared a list of the substance names in the correct categories on a large sheet of paper. Allow approximately 20 minutes for this stage.

On a second large sheet of paper the teacher then asks the group to list how particular substances from the previous exercise are viewed, i.e., which substances are viewed as acceptable to use and which are not acceptable. There are four categories for this.

— *Acceptable to Use*	— *Not Acceptable to Use*
— Legal to Use	— Illegal to Use

Again, allow 20 minutes for this stage. Finally, facilitate a group discussion on the issues raised and on the different ideas and attitudes of the students.

Learning Activity 6 RISK REDUCTION IN SUBSTANCE USE

This Learning Activity is intended to make students aware of how substance use may be related to HIV infection and how the risks can be minimized.

Begin by explaining to the group how HIV transmission can be related to substance use. Taking substances and getting effects from that substance can often alter the judgement and behaviour of a person. This may lead to forms of unsafe sexual behaviour (which is covered in *Learning Activity* 3). In addition, the way in which substances are used can also influence the risk of HIV transmission, e.g., injecting equipment can easily become contaminated when shared with others.

The instructor writes down the following methods of substance administration on six large pieces of paper:

— *ingestion*	— *sucking or chewing*
— *inhalation*	— sniffing
— intravenous injection	— other modes of injections

Stick the six sheets of paper on the wall, some distance apart. Then call out a substance name, e.g., tobacco, and ask the students to write the name of that substance under any of the headings describing a way in which that substance can be taken. Repeat the exercise with different substance names, e.g., cocaine, opium, alcohol, cannabis, etc.

The teacher then facilitates a discussion on the lists of substances and methods of administration and mistakes are rectified.

Next, stick two signs on the wall, some distance apart, one sign saying SAFE and the other sign *UNSAFE.* Ask the students to arrange the sheets of paper with the substance names and routes of administration on them in between the signs according to whether they think substances are *safe* or *unsafe* to take in terms of HIV transmission. If no one can guess where a route of administration should go, the teacher should pin it up.

Finally, the teacher should move any headed sheets of paper that are clearly in the wrong place. The teacher then facilitates a discussion on safer drug use and explains that injecting substances and sharing injecting equipment is unsafe and can lead to the transmission of bloodborne pathogens like HIV. Some risks associated with substance use can be reduced by taking the substance by a different route of administration. The teacher should encourage students to avoid giving moralistic answers and it may be that some people will not be able to change their behaviour. The emphasis is on safer use and reducing harm. Allow 25 minutes for this final session.

NURSING CARE OF THE ADULT WITH HIV-RELATED ILLNESS

GENERAL OBJECTIVES

On completion of this module, the student will be able to identify nursing interventions designed to meet the physical and psychosocial needs of the adult with symptomatic HIV related illness.

SPECIFIC OBJECTIVES

On completion of this module, the student should be able to:

- identify the acute and chronic physical problems associated with HIV infection and plan meaningful nursing interventions.
- describe the nursing implications of available medical treatments for the range of common opportunistic diseases associated with HIV infection seen in their own community.
- discuss the concept of case management and the role of the nurse in enabling patients to be cared for at home.
- develop a nursing care plan based on the availability of local facilities and resources to meet the physical, emotional, financial and social needs of people with HIV/AIDS.

INTRODUCTION

The nursing care of the person with HIV-related illness is the same as the nursing care which is assessed, planned, implemented and evaluated for any person who is ill. Consequently, all trained nurses are competent to care for patients with HIV-related illness as the same principles of nursing practice apply. In addition, many of the health care problems people will have as a result of HIV infection will be familiar to nurses because of their knowledge and experience of caring for people with other chronic, progressive diseases.

To further expand the competence and confidence of nurses caring for individuals infected with HIV, this module will provide them with an opportunity to become familiar with the range of opportunistic diseases (discussed in *Module 2*) seen in their own community and the health care needs of people with these diseases. It will also present an opportunity to discuss the nursing implications of locally available medical treatment. Infection control issues, i.e., the concept of *universal precautions*, discussed in detail in Module 3, are further reinforced in this module and nurses are reminded that any infection control precautions judged to be appropriate for nursing individuals known to be infected with HIV are equally applicable in all clinical settings, with all patients, all the time.

LEARNING ACTIVITIES

Learning Activities Key (Module 7)

Learning Activity 1	Nursing Interventions in Symptomatic HIV infection
Learning Activity 2	Opportunistic Disease
Learning Activity 3	Community *Case Management*
Learning Activity 4	Case Presentation of Symptomatic HIV Infection

Learning Activity 1 NURSING INTERVENTIONS IN SYMPTOMATIC HIV INFECTION

This activity is intended to familiarize students with the broad range of potential health care problems commonly seen in symptomatic HIV infection in order for them to develop increased skills in appropriate nursing interventions.

The format of a large group discussion is used so that students can contribute and discuss possible interventions. This will enable the instructor to draw upon the considerable expertise which already exists within the group, and to reinforce the point that the student's current competencies, practice skills and knowledge are sufficient to enable them to assess, plan, implement and evaluate meaningful nursing care for people with symptomatic HIV infection.

On a board in front of the class, list the following health care problems. As each problem is listed, ask the students to describe:

- the nursing assessment and observations relevant to that specific health care problem
- appropriate nursing interventions that might be planned for a person with that particular health care problem.

The students' responses should be written on the board as they are made and the instructor can supply and list additional relevant information if it is not forthcoming from the group.

Important:

No comprehensive list of nursing interventions is given in the following list because cultural and geographical factors, accepted practices, and the availability of resources will vary between regions. However, the instructor should review the following list and add or delete as appropriate.

COMMON HEALTH CARE PROBLEMS IN SYMPTOMATIC HIV INFECTION

PROBLEM	*POSSIBLE CAUSE*
ANOREXIA	Commonly seen in end-stage disease, sometimes complicated by nausea and vomiting (N.B. may be a side-effect of some agents used in medical treatment).
DEPENDENCE	May be caused by chronic disease progression, weakness, or neurological impairment (physical and/or cognitive).
DIARRHOEA	Often chronic and severe, it can make the person house-bound or confined to bed. It may cause significant weight loss and may bę life threatening because of dehydration and electrolyte imbalance.
DYSPHAGIA	Frequently caused by oesophageal candidiasis.
DYSPNOEA	Chest infections, anaemia.
MALNUTRITION	May be due to dysphagia, anorexia or malabsorption or inadequate intake of nutrients (especially protein). Severe weight loss (e.g., wasting syndrome or Slim disease) often seen in end-stage disease.
NEUROLOGICAL IMPAIRMENT	This may have physical and cognitive aspects: *Physical*: Lack of fine motor co-ordination, periplexal neuropathy, ataxia, dysphasia, visual impairment and blindness, loss of hearing, paralysis. *Cognitive*: Memory loss, slowed thinking, confusion, poor processing of information, personality changes, dementia.
OEDEMA	May be due to lymph node enlargement as a result of Kaposi sarcoma.
PYREXIA	Continuous or intermittent, often low-grade, rising during periods of acute infection and sometimes associated with night sweats.
SKIN LESIONS	May be caused by a variety of skin problems, e.g. Candida, Kaposi sarcoma, Herpes simplex/zoster, etc. Lesions often involve mucous membranes.
VISUAL PROBLEMS	Frequently seen in retinitis caused by cytomegalovirus (CMV) or may be neurological in origin.

N.B. This is not meant to bean exclusive list of all health care problems commonly seen in *people* with symptomatic HIV infection . The instructor is encouraged to adapt this list to *local* experiences of caring for patients with symptomatic HIV infection.

Learning Activity 2 OPPORTUNISTIC DISEASE

The instructor should briefly review the material in *Module 2* in relation to opportunistic diseases. In this Learning Activity, the instructor introduces each of the opportunistic diseases listed below in the context of a large group discussion and explains the usual clinical presentation of each condition. Students should be invited to give suggestions about the actual and potential nursing care needs that might be associated with each particular opportunistic condition. List each of the opportunistic diseases on the board or on large sheets of paper, together with any associated nursing care needs which students suggest (identify separately *actual* and *potential nursing* care needs, i.e., patient problems).

OPPORTUNISTIC CONDITIONS RELATED TO HIV INFECTION

OPPORTUNISTIC DISEASE	*HEALTH CARE NEEDS (PROBLEMS)*

- Pneurnonia caused by:
  - *Mycobacterium tuberculosis*
  - *Pneumocystis carinii*
  - Cytomegalovirus
  - Atypical mycobacteria
  - Lymphoid interstitial pneumonitis

- Oral and/or oesophageal candidiasis
- Kaposi sarcoma
- Recurrent bacterial and viral infections
- *Herpes zoster* infections
- Generalized lymphadenopathy
- *Herpes simplex* infections
- Neurological impairment
- Wasting disease (e.g. "Slim")
- Gastrointestinal infections (e.g. *Cryptospordia)*
- Neurological infections (e.g. *Cryptococcus neoformans, Toxoplasma gondii)*
- Lymphoma
- Cytomegalovirus infection

N.B. *The above is not an "exclusive" list of common opportunistic conditions and the instructor is encouraged to adapt this list appropriately to their own local* experiences of the clinical manifestations of symptomatic HIV infection.

Following the above class presentation and discussion, divide the students into 4 small groups and assign 2 to 3 opportunistic diseases, along with the actual and potential health care needs (patient problems) identified. Instruct each group to design a nursing care plan directed at preventing potential problems from being realized and at implementing effective nursing management for actual problems identified. Allow 30 to 45 minutes for small group work and then re-form the group for a final session and discuss the nursing management for each of the opportunistic diseases discussed.

Learning Activity 3 COMMUNITY CASE MANAGEMENT

This Learning Activity gives the students the opportunity to consider the relative advantages and disadvantages of people being cared for in a variety of settings, e.g., in hospital, in out-patient clinics and/or in the home. This activity builds on the work completed earlier in this module and the students will find it useful to refer to their notes from Learning Activities I and 2.

HOSPITAL CLINIC AND HOME CARE

Nursing care includes patient education (see *Module* 6), counselling (see *Module 5)* and case management. Case management may be defined as the assessment of the patients needs by the key worker to enable the coordination of the resources that may be used to meet those needs. To be able to help decide which setting might provide the most effective use of resources for each individual patient, it is necessary to remember the possible disadvantages associated with each option, e.g.:

In-patient care in a hospital - some of the possible disadvantages might be:

- may not be appropriate
- may not be available
- may be too expensive
- may be rejected by the patient
- may be too far away from the patients home and family.

Care in an out-patient clinic some of the possible disadvantages might be:

- may not be available
- may be too for away from home
- may not be held often enough
- may have long waiting times.

Home-based care some of the possible disadvantages might be:

- shortage of care-givers
- lack of home nursing resources
- patient may not have a home
- places continuous demand on other family members
- other members of the family may also be sick.

However, each of the above also has distinct advantages, e.g. hospitals are often the ideal setting for the investigation and treatment of acute disease, while out-patient clinics can often support patients who might otherwise require in-patient care in hospital.

Home-based care is often the only option available or the option most desired by the patient. It is a possible alternative to hospital or clinic care if:

- there is a support system to provide care, e.g. family, partner, friends
- the nurse can provide teaching and support

— the patient prefers to spend the terminal phase of their illness at home
— the patient is comfortable and confident about home care.

The instructor should divide the class into 4 small groups and ask them to review the common health care problems identified in *Learning Activity 1* and the appropriate nursing intervention for each of those problems. Each group will also need to review the health care needs identified in *Learning Activity 2*. Following this review, each group will need to focus on the following questions:

- How might the nursing interventions identified in Learning Activity 1 be implemented in the home setting?
- What teaching and support would be necessary to enable the extended family or friends to provide care for a person at home?
- What local clinical resources are available to support nurses caring for patients in their own homes?

Reform the class and ask each group leader to report back in plenary session.

Learning Activity 4 CASE STUDY OF SYMPTOMATIC HIV INFECTION

In this Learning Activity, the students are provided with a *Case Presentation* which raises the major issues that might need to be dealt with when caring for a patient with symptomatic HIV infection.

The class should be divided into 4 small groups and each group should be given a copy of the case study. The students should be asked to read it, to assess and identify the nursing care needs of the patient and to answer the questions which follow each section. Group leaders should report back in a plenary class discussion. Instructors are encouraged to adapt or develop their own *Case Presentations* which may more appropriately present the nursing care needs of patients in their own communities, who are being cared for at home.

Case Study—Part A

Mrs. P is a 28 year-old woman who lives with her husband and three children in a village outside a large city. Her husband is a truck driver who is absent three or four days a week. Her mother lives nearby. Mrs. P has not felt well for the past year and her mother has frequently taken care of the two younger children during the day and the older child after school. Mrs. P has no appetite, has had diarrhoea and has gradually lost 10 kilograms in weight. She thought she had intestinal parasites, a common problem in her village, so six months ago she went to the health clinic where she was treated for parasites. However, since then the diarrhoea has become more frequent and the lymph nodes in her neck are swollen and tender. She has fevers nearly every evening and wakes up during the night soaked with sweat. This week, she has white patches in her mouth and a sore throat. When she swallows, she has a burning feeling in her chest just beneath her ribs. She is dehydrated. You are seeing her at the district health centre.

IDENTIFY THE NURSING ARE NEEDS OF MRS. P

- What additional information do you think you need to ask Mrs. P in order to decide what action to take? What do you suspect is the underlying medical reason for Mrs. P's many different problems?
- What immediate nursing care needs and interventions would you implement for her?
- What nursing support would Mrs. P require in relation to any potential emotional or social issues she may have to cope with?
- What referrals or further investigations might be appropriate and available?

Case Study—Part B

Mrs. P is admitted to the hospital and rehydrated. A scraping of her tongue reveals oral candidiasis. The doctor thinks that she also has oesophageal candidiasis because of the burning feeling in her chest and her difficulty in swallowing. Nystatin tablets are prescribed and she is also given nystatin suspension to swill around her mouth for the oral candidiasis.
Stool specimens are taken and are negative for parasites, but positive for acid first bacilli (AFB). Blood studies reveal anuemia and the presence of AFB. The doctor asks Mrs. P for consent to have a blood test for HIV antibodies and explains the reasons why he feels this test is necessary. He also very carefully explains to Mrs. P what a positive and a negative result might mean. After careful thought, Mrs. P agrees to have the HIV antibody test. This test is positive for HIV antibodies.
A chest x-ray does not demonstrate pulmonary tuberculosis (TB) and the doctor explains that the positive AFB in the stool and blood specimens are probably the result of atypical mycobacterial infection *(Mycobacterium* avium-intercellulare, MAI), i.e., MAI and not tuberculosis. He prescribes ethambutol and streptomycin which may control MAI. The doctor writes this in the chart and asks you to accompany him when he tells Mrs. P. that her diagnosis is AIDS. Mrs. P is extremely upset and wants her mother contacted immediately.

IDENTIFY THE NURSING ARE NEEDS OF MRS. P

- What specific information indicates to the doctor that Mrs. P has AIDS?
- What should the nurse know about the administration and possible side-effects of the medications prescribed by the doctor?
- What counselling interventions will you plan to help Mrs. P cope with her diagnosis?
- What are her educational needs in relation to her anaemia and weight loss and how will you plan to help meet these needs?

Case Study—Part C

Mrs. P has received the medications for two weeks. The candida is no longer a problem and the diarrhoea is much better with only one loose stool per day. She has gained 5 kilograms and is feeling much stronger. The doctor is ready to discharge her to her home. She is to continue taking ethambutol and streptomycin and to continue to use the nystatin suspension to keep her oral candidiasis under control. Mrs. P says she is worried that she will infect her children or that her neighbours will tell her to leave the village.

IDENTIFY THE NURSING CARE NEEDS OF MRS. P

- What are the educational needs of Mrs. P prior to her safe discharge home and how will the nurse meet these needs?
- Mrs. P is particularly worried about infecting her children and husband and asks the nurse if it is safe to cook for her family and can she still have sexual relations with her husband; how does the nurse respond?
- Is there anything the nurse can do to help Mrs. P in relation to her fears that her neighbours will reject her and force her to leave the village?

Case Study—Part D

Mrs. P returns home and her condition is stable for two months, although she has started to lose weight again. Then she begins to weaken and to have more severe symptoms. You make a home visit from the clinic. Mrs. P does not want to return to the hospital because travelling to and from the clinic has been very hard on her husband (who is now also unwell) and her mother. She thinks she will probably die and cries when she thinks about leaving her children and her husband. She wonders what will happen to her children if her husband (who she thinks also has AIDS) dies, as her mother is very old now.

IDENTIFY THE NURSING CARE NEEDS OF MRS. P

What can you teach Mrs. P's mother and husband to enable them to care for her at home? What are you able to do to provide emotional support for Mrs. P? What will you tell her when she asks you to help explain to her husband that she knows she is going to die and wants to die at home? What support is available locally to Mrs. P to die at home? What resources are locally available to care for Mrs. P is children if her husband becomes ill and also dies and Mrs. P's mother is no longer able to cope?

THE IMPACT OF HIV INFECTION AND HIV-RELATED ILLNESS ON WOMEN

GENERAL OBJECTIVE

On completion of this module the student will have gained an understanding of the possible risk to women of HIV infection and acquired an ability to anticipate the pre-natal and postnatal needs of women related to HIV infection.

SPECIFIC OBJECTIVES

On completion of this module the student should be able:

- to identify the risks of HIV infection to which a woman and her unborn child may be exposed
- to describe the influences in society which may put women at risk of acquiring HIV infection
- to discuss the health education and counselling needs of women who may be at risk of HIV infection
- to describe the effects of HIV infection and HIV-related illnesses on a pregnant woman and her unborn baby
- to implement safe practices related to the care of women during pregnancy and childbirth, applicable to any setting
- to develop teaching strategies for traditional birth attendants and pregnant women, related to reducing the risk of HIV infection.

INTRODUCTION

This module addresses the particular risks of HIV infection that women may face and their vulnerability due to their role and status in society. The effects of HIV infection on pregnancy are considered as is the challenge the infection poses for the mother, her unborn child and those involved in their care.

LEARNING ACTIVITY

LEARNING ACTIVITY KEY (MODULE 8)

Learning *Activity 1* Women in Society
Learning *Activity 2* Health Education and Counselling Needs of Women
Learning *Activity 3* The Pregnant Woman and HIV Infection
Learning *Activity 4* Assessment of Safe Working Practices

Learning Activity 1 provides students with opportunities to examine the position and role of women in society and how these may influence the risk of HIV infection for women.

Learning Activity 2 focuses on the health education needs of women and appropriate health education strategies to meet these needs. It also considers the choices available to women, which may be discussed in a counselling situation.

Learning Activity 3 addresses the implications of HIV infection, related to pregnancy, childbirth and the postnatal period and discusses safe practices, applicable to any setting.

Learning Activity 4 describes strategies for teaching safe clinical practice in midwifery to midwives and traditional birth attendants.

Background Information

Women's vulnerability to HIV infection is directly related to their status in society, including social and cultural expectations about their sexuality. In addition, they carry a much greater burden than men in terms of the social and cultural impact of the pandemic, not least because of their traditional role as care-givers. WHO is currently developing a strategy to assist member States to develop a national plan which will more effectively address the impact of HIV infection and AIDS on women. This strategy will include objectives such as:

- reducing women's vulnerability to HIV/AIDS related to socio-economic status, e.g. by increasing their social, economic, legal and political status and providing and strengthening programmes and services which meet their needs.
- reducing the incidence of HIV infection (and other sexually transmitted diseases) in women, e.g., by reducing their biological and social vulnerability to HIV infection and other sexually transmitted diseases, and reducing their vulnerability to the bloodborne transmission of HIV.
- reducing the social and cultural impact of HIV infection and AIDS on women, e.g., by increasing women's ability to determine their own HIV status, and their access to health care, and to enable them to decide upon their own family planning options and reduce their care-giving burden.

Learning Activity 1 WOMEN IN SOCIETY

The instructor should review with the class the routes of HIV transmission, i.e., sex, transfer of infected blood and blood products and perinatal (vertical) transmission. List these routes on the board and ask the class to identify in which ways women in particular may be exposed to infection. List these on the board.

The students should then be divided into small groups to consider the following questions:

1. Traditionally, what is a woman's role in this society? What are the advantages and disadvantages of being a woman in this society?
2. How does the status and role of women affect a woman's ability to:
   a) control her own fertility and obtain contraception?
   b) have access to health care?
   c) negotiate safer sex?

Issues arising from this may include traditional customs and taboos related to the role of women, inequality between men and women and lack of power, effects of poverty and prostitution, lack of education for women, high cost and poor availability of contraception, and poor health care, especially related to pregnancy and childbirth.

From the feedback (leaving the list on the board) and referring back to the routes of transmission, the instructor should lead the class discussion on to identifying the specific HIV-related risks to which women are exposed. This may be discussed in terms of the following:

- Women who have unprotected sex with
  i) a partner who has other sex contact
  ii) many sexual partners
  iii) someone who has a sexually transmitted disease
- Women who have unprotected anal intercourse
- Women who have received blood transfusions in the past
- Women who are injecting drug users or who are the partners of injecting drug users.

Learning Activity 2 HEALTH EDUCATION AND COUNSELLING NEEDS OF WOMEN

Health education needs of women

The instructor should remind the class of the content of *Module* 6 which will be applied in this section specifically to women. In

Module 6 the students considered patterns of sexual behaviour in their community and what might be the barriers to effective education and risk reduction for patients in a health care setting. The instructor should remind the class that education is a vital aspect of preventing HIV/ AIDS. Education is essential because it can affect the health of the whole family and society. The class will be considering the particular educational needs of women.

Using a board or a large piece of paper, the instructor will ask the class to identify the specific health education needs of women in their society in relation to HIV infection and AIDS. Possible needs identified might include:

- Knowledge of what the disease is and how the virus is transmitted, especially among woman and children.
- Knowledge about the effects of HIV in women and children.
- How transmission of the virus can be prevented in woman and children.

Health education strategies

Divide the class into groups of 6 to 8, consisting if possible of students with related duties or common interests.

Each group has the task of devising a health education initiative, related to one of the areas of needs they have identified. They must take into account the possible barriers to health education specifically related to women [see *Module* 6], as well as issues such as access and resources.

Possible strategies might involve using local community groups, traditional women's groups, maternal and child health clinics or other health care outlets, as well as through media particularly targeted towards women.

Each group will summarize their discussion and present their strategy to the rest of the class.

Counselling needs of women In relation to HIV Infection

As well as group health education initiatives, it is important to consider the needs of women on an individual basis, especially if they feel they have been in situations associated with an increased risk of HIV exposure. The section will consider possible strategies for counselling women individually. Students should review *Module 5* before undertaking this section.

The purpose of the section is to enable students to consider the possible choices open to a woman who has, or may have been, exposed to the risk of HIV infection.

The teacher can refer to *Module 6* for possible teaching strategies. One suggested method is to ask the class to divide into pairs. They are then given a brief case history of a woman who believes that she has been at risk of HIV infection. They are to consider the possible realistic options open to her. The pair should discuss the issues from the viewpoints of the nurse (or health worker) and the patient. The pairs will then return to the class for feedback . The teacher should list the options from the health worker' s and the patient' s viewpoints separately. Depending on the size of the group, each pair can consider all the options or an individual.

The Options for the Patient May Include:

HAVING AN HIV ANTIBODY TEST..

THIS OPTION, SEEN FROM THE HEALTH WORKER'S VIEWPOINT

- enables him/her to make informed decisions about the management of patient and family
- he/she must consider the consequences to the patient and family and the possible support they will need
- the availability and cost of the test must be taken into account.

THIS OPTION, SEEN FROM THE CLIENT/PATIENTS VIEWPOINT

- enables her to make informed decisions about her future and her family
- should also include consideration of:
  - the impact on her relationship with others e.g., her husband and/or family, irrespective of the result
  - possible future support she will need
  - the access to health care
  - the impact on her role/job in society.

NOT HAVING AN HIV ANTIBODY TEST..

THIS OPTION, SEEN FROM THE HEALTH WORKER'S VIEWPOINT, CAUSES

- continued uncertainty about the management of the patient and family
- inability to give appropriate support and advice.

WHILE FROM THE PATIENTS POINT OF VIEW, THERE IS

- continued anxiety and uncertainty
- the impact on her relationships with others, e.g., her husband and/ or other members of her family, etc.

IF THE TEST IS POSITIVE AND SHE IS PREGNANT...

THE HEALTH WORKER'S VIEW MIGHT FOCUS ON

- advice to the woman in relation to what is known about perinatal transmission and possible consequences to the woman of continuing the pregnancy
- legislation and local attitudes/beliefs related to abortion
- the health care support the woman will need if the pregnancy continues
- confidentiality and issues related to the family.

THE PATIENT'S VIEW MIGHT ENCOMPASS

— understanding the consequences to herself and the child of continuing with the pregnancy
— patient's beliefs and attitudes to abortion and the woman's role in childbearing
— husband's and families reaction to abortion
— her personal or cultural need and/or to have descendants
— possible future health care and support needs.

The feedback from the pairs should be followed by a discussion on the role of the nurse/ health worker in these situations and on the practical help which they are able to offer.

- counselling
- referral:
  — to HIV counsellor
  — to midwife
  — for contraceptive advice
  — to obstetrician/gynaecologist
  — for advice on safer sex
  — for information on health care facilities and resources.

Learning Activity 3 THE PREGNANT WOMAN AND HIV INFECTION

The purpose of this section is to discuss the implications of HIV infection and HIV-related illness in pregnancy and during the postpartum period and the assessment of the pregnant and postpartum woman.

The instructor should present the following material to the class:

HIV Infection and Pregnancy

Women who are infected with HIV may transmit the virus to their babies during pregnancy, during delivery and through breast feeding. This risk varies according to a number off actors. These factors include whether the mother was seropositive before her pregnancy (or became infected during the pregnancy) and her immunological and health status during the pregnancy Current data suggest that the risk of an HIV positive mother infecting her unborn child is approximately 30%.

Access to prenatal counselling is often limited. Therefore, many women who are at risk are pregnant before their initial contact with a nurse or health care worker. In many areas HIV-antibody testing is not available. Even in areas where testing is possible, some HIV-positive women may wish to continue their pregnancy. If nurses and health care workers are to provide informed support for their patients, they must be aware of current information related to transmission of the virus from mother to child.

A baby can be infected through vertical transmission in the following ways:

a) In utero by transmission from an infected mother to her fetus (HIV has in some cases been found in the unborn baby after only sixteen weeks gestation)

b) During delivery
c) During breast-feeding. The WHO/UNICEF 1992 statement on HIV transmission and breast-feeding summarizes the current position relating to infant feeding (see Chapter 4).

The instructor should conclude by indicating that mother-to-baby transmission of HIV has an impact at a personal level and at a broader level, in that it affects future generations.

Assessment of the pregnant woman

Present this short case history to the class either using handouts or by writing it on the board. You can adapt the case history according to local circumstances.

Case History

Mrs. T. is a 19 year-old woman, who is 6 months pregnant with her first baby.
She attends the maternal and child health clinic for the first time. She says that she feels tired, does not appear to be gaining weight and is breathless when she walks.
There is a high prevalence of HIV infection in the area.

Divide the class into groups of 6 to 8. Ask each group to discuss how they would assess this patient, how they might clarify the diagnosis and what advice they would give her.

Ask the students to address the following questions in their discussion:

1. What are the possible causes of her condition?
2. What questions would they ask her, which might help them find out what is wrong?
3. What tests might be carried out to assist in the diagnosis?
4. What advice would they give her?

Summarize on the board the feedback from each group. Possible responses to each question are summarized below:

---

1. CAUSES

Anaemia due to:

— malnutrition
— malaria
— HIV-related illness
— worm infestation
— tuberculosis
— Sickle cell disease

2. QUESTIONS

General health history including:

— duration of illness
— incidence of other diseases in the family (HIV infection, Tuberculosis)
— recent attacks of malaria

3. TESTS

— Chest X-ray
— Haemoglobin and full blood count
— Sickle cell test
— Microscopy of stool sample
— Microscopy of sputum sample
— HIV antibody test

4. ADVICE

— rest
— explanation about HIV infection and AIDS
— information on good nutrition
— advice on safer sex/personal hygiene
— encourage regular attendance at clinic to monitor condition
— to enlist family support

Conclude by emphasizing the importance of careful assessment to provide early recognition of HIV infection and other conditions, and the importance of appropriate treatment and support.

Learning Activity 4 ASSESSMENT OF SAFE WORKING PRACTICES DURING CHILDBIRTH

Ask the class to divide into small groups. Give each group a fictional case history, which illustrates one of the situations below, or develop situations which they are likely to encounter in their practice.

Some situations may present problems relating to inadequate resources or to the large quantities of blood involved. There are no easy answers as to how nurses or midwives can protect themselves from coming into contact with blood during labour and delivery. The basic guidelines presented in *Module 3* must be followed.

The following is a list of situations which could be illustrated by a fictional case history:

1. Childbirth in hospital where sterile conditions for delivery are available
2. A home delivery by a midwife in a house with hot running water, a gas stove and a toilet (a water closet)
3. A home delivery by a traditional birth affendant in a house

with water carried from a well, a wood fire for heat and a pit latrine for a toilet.

Ask each group to refer to the guidelines identified in *Module 3* for the prevention of HIV transmission in health care settings, and to develop appropriate strategies for the assigned situations based on the guidelines. Ask the students to consider:

a) How would a delivery normally be conducted in these circumstances?
b) The risks to which the attendant will be exposed and why (e.g., contact with blood)
c) How these risks could be minimized.

Areas which should be considered include:

- examination of the woman during labour
- position for delivery
- rupture of the fetal membranes
- bleeding from vaginal tears and episiotomy
- contact with urine and faeces
- handling the baby
- cutting the umbilical cord and cord care
- examination and disposal of the placenta.

Exposure to Blood

The process of labour and delivery may involve extensive contact with blood. Because this entails the risk of HIV infection, precautions should be taken to minimize contact with the mother's blood by the baby and by those attending the mother. These precautions may include using barriers such as gloves, though these may not be available in many settings. Some practices associated with labour and delivery are shaped by tradition and may involve risk to others by exposing them to blood. Such practices could be changed to lessen exposure.

When the students have completed this activity (about 45 minutes) ask each group to report back its findings. Have the class discuss each presentation, the precautions and strategies that have been suggested.

Complete the activity by discussing:

1. How do nurses and midwives who have inadequate resources cope with fears of becoming infected?
2. What measures can nurses and midwives take to ensure that they have the resources to deliver babies safely?

Remind the class that the same principles and precautions apply to the continuing care of mother and baby after delivery.

NURSING CARE OF THE INFANT OR CHILD WITH HIV-RELATED ILLNESS

GENERAL OBJECTIVE

On completion of this module, the student will be able to describe the clinical consequences of HIV infection in children and initiate interventions to meet the nursing care needs of both the affected child and his/her family,

SPECIFIC OBJECTIVES

On completion of this module the student should be able:

- to identify ways in which infants and children can be exposed to HIV
- to recognize the signs and symptoms of HIV-related illness in children, with reference to either the CDC or WHO classification systems
- to plan appropriate nursing care for the affected child and relevant support for the family

INTRODUCTION

As the majority of children with HIV infection and HIV-related illness become infected by perinatal (vertical) transmission, nurses are often caring for the entire family (many members of which are sick or dying) presenting problems of diminishing social support for the sick child. In addition, HIV-related illness in children are different from that seen in adults. Nurses will need to be able to differentiate between paediatric HIV-related illness and other common illnesses seen in children in order to plan appropriate nursing interventions.

Learning Activity 1 reviews the possible means of HIV transmission in children and the feelings this may create for those affected.

Learning Activity 2 explores the clinical consequences of HIV infection in children and describes two common classification systems used to stage paediatric HIV infection.

Learning Activity 3 facilitates the development of skills in assessing, planning, implementing and evaluating nursing care for affected children and their families.

Learning Activity 1 HIV TRANSMISSION IN INFANTS AND CHILDREN

The purpose of this exercise is to identify and explore reactions to HIV infection and the special issues it raises within affected families. A broad range of powerful feelings and anxieties will be seen, from guilt at infecting someone else (e.g., husband transmitting HIV to his wife, mother infecting her child, etc.), fear for the future (who will take care of the children if the mother and father become ill or die?), to hopelessness and despair.

Begin this session by reviewing appropriate information from *Modules I and 8* and focus on the background information below.

Transmission of HIV to Children

Most children infected with HIV, including those with AIDS, have become infected during pregnancy during or shortly after birth (i.e., vertical transmission). HIV infection can occur before birth (in utero infection) after only 15 weeks gestation. Infection can also occur during delivery (intrapartum infection) when the infant is exposed to infected maternal birth fluids. Virus may be present in cervical secretions and there is the added risk of exchange of blood between mother and child during birth. Infants may also be infected after birth (postpartum infection). Infection from the ingestion of breast milk has been described in several cases where mothers acquired their infection shortly after birth from a blood transfusion. Children can also become infected following transfusion of HIV-contaminated blood or blood products. The use of non-sterile equipment in health care facilities or by traditional practitioners may also expose children to the risk of HIV infection. Additionally, children maybe infected following sexual exposure to the virus or exposure from injecting drug use practices. Finally, in cultures where adolescent children (aged 13 to 18 years) have their first sexual experience with a prostitute, or where child prostitution or sexual abuse of children is common, there will be added risks for children.

Following presentation of this information to the class, have them discuss the most common means by which infants or children are infected with HIV in their local community. List each transmission mode on the blackboard and, with reference to *Modules 6* and 8, review strategies for the primary prevention of HIV infection in infants and children. Then divide the class into small groups and ask them to discuss the following questions:

What thoughts and fears might:

- a mother who is infected with HIV have for her 4 month-old child?
- a parent have for his/her child who received a blood transfusion?
- a 12 year-old prostitute, who works on the streets of your nearest city, have on discovering that he/she is infected with HIV?
- a family of four, two infected with HIV and two not infected, have?

Allow 30 minutes for small group discussions and then have each group report back to the class.

After the small groups report back, list the issues on the board and discuss with the class where nursing intervention may be useful, e.g. counselling, advice on health care facilities, referral to appropriate agencies for fostering or adoption and secondary and tertiary prevention. Complete this Learning Activity by presenting the following information to the class.

Mother-To-Fetus/Infant Transmission

The transmission rate of HIV infection from mother-to-fetus/infant during pregnancy at time of delivery and through breast-feeding is approximately 30%.

The risk of HIV transmission through breast-feeding must be weighed against the well recognized immunological, nutritional, psychological and contraceptive benefits of breast milk and/or breast-feeding {see WHO Guidelines on Breast-Feeding in Chapter 14.

It is difficult to determine whether a newborn infant is HIV-infected. In HIV-infected women, maternal HIV antibody is passively transmitted across the placenta to the fetus during pregnancy. This antibody can persist in the infant new born infant for as long as 18 months. Conseaquently, during this period, the detection of HIV antibody in infants does not necessarily mean that an infant is infected.

Tests for the direct detection of HIV, e.g. through virus culture, polymerase chain reaction (PCR) are becoming available. These tests can determine the child's HIV infection status more definitively. However, they are both very costly and complex to perform.

Conclude by answering any questions or further clarifying any points raised in discussion.

Learning Activity 2 HIV-RELATED ILLNESS IN INFANTS AND CHILDREN

Begin this Learning Activity by asking anyone in the group with experience in caring for infants or children with HIV infection to describe to the class what health care needs such children had. Follow on from this brief introduction to the session by presenting the following background information.

HIV-Related Illness in Infants and Children

The most common symptoms of HIV infection in children are:

- *weight loss*
- *failure to thrive*
- *fever*
- *chronic diarrhoea*
- *oral thrush*

Oral thrush, which often recurs after treatment, can be the first indication of HIV infection.

HIV-infected children have an increased frequency of common paediatric infections, such as ear infections and pneumonia. In developing countries, other diseases, such as chronic gastroenteritis and tuberculosis, are also frequent in these children. In addition, the symptoms common to many treatable diseases tend to be more persistent and severe in HIV-infected infants, e.g. recurrent fever, diarrhoea and generalized dermatitis. Moreover, HIV-infected infants do not respond as well to treatment of these conditions and are more likely to suffer life-threatening complications.

Enlarged lymph nodes and an enlarged liver are common in children infected with HIV. As HIV infection progresses, opportunistic diseases also begin to appear. Finally, many, if not most, of these children have some type of neurological involvement, such as developmental delay or encephalopathy. The majority of infected infants develop disease early in life and have a high mortality.

Diagnostic Criteria for AIDS in Infants

Following the presentation of the above background information to the class, refer students to the national AIDS definition. Remind students that this definition is for epidemiological surveillance purposes and not for the purpose of clinical care management. The diagnosis of paediatric AIDS is difficult. In addition, in developing countries, diagnostic procedures, such as the polymerase chain reaction and virus culture, are not routinely performed. The following WHO Clinical Case Definition was developed and is used in many developing countries.

WHO Clinical case definition of paediatric AIDS

The presence of any two major and any two minor signs from those listed below, in the absence of other known causes of immunodeficiency:

MAJOR SIGNS

(1) Weight loss or abnormally slow growth
(2) Chronic diarrhoea for more than one month
(3) Prolonged or intermittent fever for more than one month.

MINOR SIGNS

(1) Generalized lymph node enlargement
(2) Oropharyngeal candidiasis (oral thrush)
(3) Recurrent common infections (otitis, pharyngitis)
(4) Persistent cough
(5) Generalized dermatitis
(6) Confirmed maternal HIV infection.

The instructor can supply additional information on the clinical presentation of paediatric HIV infection in their own country. It is important that students have an understanding of the concept of opportunistic diseases which result once the immune system becomes depressed following HIV infection. Presenting opportunistic infections may vary in different countries of the world and are partly determined by the background of common infectious agents to which children are exposed.

Conclude this Learning Activity by discussing how a competent nursing assessment will identify health care needs in children with HIV-related illness.

Learning Activity 8 PLANNING NURSING CARE

Introduce this session by reviewing the common health care needs in children with HIV infection that were identified in *Learning Activity* 2. Then present the following background information:

Care Recommendations for Children with HIV-Related Illness

The following general recommendations should be used in the management of HIV positive infants and in teaching their mothers and care-givers during counselling.

MAINTAIN GOOD NUTRITIONAL STATUS

In most circumstances, HIV-infected mothers should be encouraged to breast-feed their infants. These mothers should also be taught appropriate weaning practices for the introduction of solid foods at 4-6 months, as well as encouraged to continue to breast-feed for up to 18-24 months. In addition, regular growth monitoring (preferably every month) is an appropriate way to monitor nutritional status. If growth falters, additional investigations should be done to determine the cause.

PROVIDE EARLY AND VIGOROUS THERAPY FOR COMMON PAEDIATRIC INFECTIONS

All infants with HIV antibodies should be treated vigorously for common paediatric infections, such as measles and otitis media. Because the immune systems of children with HIV infection are often impaired, these diseases may be more persistent and severe, and the children may respond poorly to therapy and develop severe complications. Conseaquently, the mothers of all HIV antibody-positive infants should be encouraged to take their infants for examination and treatment as soon as possible, whenever symptoms develop.

IMMUNIZE ACCORDING TO STANDARD SCHEDULES

All infants and chilc 'en should be immunized according to standard schedules. The only exception is that infants with clinical symptoms of HIV infection should not be given tuberculosis vaccine (BCG). It is important that sterilization procedures for immunization equipment be strictly followed, to prevent transmission of a variety of infectious agents, including HIV.

ENSURE THE CHILD HAS A GOOD QUALITY OF LIFE

Most infants of HIV-infected mothers are not infected with HIV. In addition, many of those who are infected will have months of as -& lotic life and some will live for years without symptoms. Every effort should be made by members of the child's family and by the health-care professional to help the child lead as normal a life as possible.

Following this presentation, answer any questions and clarify any issues raised by the class.

Assessing the Family's Ability to Care for a Child with HIV Infection and HIV-related Illness

In assessing the ability of the family (some of whom will also be suffering from the effects of HIV infection) to case for the child, the following questions might be helpful:

QUESTIONS

1. What is the parent's state of health, including their emotional condition? Are they physically able to care for the child?
2. What individuals can offer support to this family? What is their state of health? Are they able and willing to help care for the child?
3. What is the family's economic situation?
4. What is the condition of their living space?
5. What does the child eat?
6. What does the family know and feel about HIV infection? Do they know how HIV is transmitted and how to prevent transmission?

Have the class discuss the following questions and allow 45 minutes for this activity:

Assessing and Planning Nursing Care

Divide the class into three groups and assign each group a Case Study, from the three given below. Alternatively, the instructor is encouraged to develop their own Case Studies which may be more relevant to paediatric HIV infection and AIDS in their own community . After discussing the case, students are asked to develop a care plan to address the physical problems, and the psychosocial needs that the plan identifies. They might find it useful to follow the following format:

1. What further information is needed to assess care appropriately? What questions about the baby would you ask the mother?
2. What examination of the child would you make?
3. List the health care and psychosocial needs of the child and its family.
4. What nursing intervention would be appropriate to meet these needs?
5. How will this nursing intervention be evaluated?
6. What advice (e.g., feeding, immunization, schooling, etc.) would you give the family?

CASE STUDY 1

(a) Mrs. P. a 22 year-old woman, brings her 10 month-old baby boy, M. to the clinic. You know her because she had been considered at high risk of losing the baby at birth. She gained very little weight during pregnancy, had chronic fatigue, fevers, diarrhoea and anorexia. She was suspected of having HIV infection, which is common in young women in her area. She is bringing her baby to the clinic because she has been feeling worse herself and is afraid he may have AIDS.
You examine the baby and discover that he weighs 9.1 kilograms, which on the chart is the normal weight for an 8 month-old baby i.e., less than the weight that M. should be. A mid-arm measurement tells you that he is malnourished and his mucous membranes are pale. His arms and legs are almost limp as you hold him, with very poor muscle tone when you push on the bottom of his foot. The mother says he sucks poorly and takes very little milk.

(b) Six months later, the mother is living with her older sister, who cares for baby M because Mrs. P is in bed most of the day. Mrs. P brings baby M to the clinic because her sister has pointed out that baby M barely crawls, while her own children were walking by the time they were 12 months old. Baby M has been in the clinic with ear infections three times in the past six months, and has had thrush for a year, which goes away when treated but returns as soon as the medication (oral mycostatin suspension) is stopped.

(c) A year has passed and Mrs. P. has died of an undiagnosed wasting disease. Her sister has taken the baby and must bring him in to the clinic frequently for treatment of ear infections, thrush and now diarrhoea. At 26 months old, he is not walking but crawls short distances. She thinks he is losing his ability to crawl and losing interest in his surroundings. He has a high fever and purulent drainage from his ear. She describes an episode two days ago which you think may have been a seizure. You decide to refer him to the district hospital for examination and possible admission.

CASE STUDY 2

(a) L is a 2 year-old girl who comes to the clinic with her mother. Recently L began to cough occasionally and feels hot at night. Her mother is being treated for thrush and chronic diarrhoea, symptoms of HIV infection that she has had since being pregnant with L. She was tested at that time and found to have antibodies to HIV. She was also diagnosed with tuberculosis and given tuberculosis medication . She is afraid L has AIDS and wants her to be tested. L is given the HIV antibody test and a chest X-ray. The nurse who examines her soys L has thrush and gives her oral mycostatin suspension. After a week, the X-ray result shows pulmonary tuberculosis, and L is brought buck to be given tuberculosis medication. The HIV antibody test comes buck within one month and is confirmed positive.

(b) L is now 3 years-old and both her parents have died of AIDS. She is brought by her grandmother to the emergency room and admitted to the hospital with pneumonia. She has been coughing and has had a fever for a week. Last night she began to have difficulty in breathing. Her nailbeds are blue, her respirations are 55/minute and her heart rate is 1 50/minute. She has a high temperature, of 1 04°F/40°C.

(c) L has been treated successfully for bacterial pneumonia but the doctor says she has Iymphoid interstitial pneumonia, which is causing chronic lung disease. L can go home but has a chronic, non-productive cough, a respiratory rate that never goes below 30/ minute and a heart rate of 120/minute. She usually has a moderate fever. She has generalized lymphadenopathy, and an enlorged liver and spleen and her fingers are clubbed at the tips. The doctor tells the grandmother he does not know how long she will live but doubts it will be more than a year.

CASE STUDY 3

(a) Mrs. C, a 30 year-old woman, comes into the hospital in labour with her fourth baby. She is an intravenous drug user and appears to have taken heroin recently. Her labour is slow and the contractions weak. Finally, the baby boy is delivered by Caesarean section and weighs only 2.0 kilograms. The mother becomes septic after her surgery and dies, leaving the baby to be cared for by the nurses in the hospital.

(b) When the baby is 6 months old he weighs 4.5 kilograms. At first, he had difficulty sucking but has managed to take enough milk to gain weight. His reflexes are hypertonic and he tends to be irritable. The hospital team agrees that his symptoms suggest HIV infection. He has had several diagnostic lumbur punctures which were normal.

(c) At 18 months, the baby is still in the hospital and has had two bouts of bacterial pneumonia . He has swollen lymph nodes in his neck and under his arms, and both his liver and spleen are enlorged. His parotid glands are also swollen. There is no reason for him to be in the hospital, but there is nobody to take responsibility for him.

Allow 60 minutes for small group discussion and then have each small group present their report and care plan to the class. Summarize and clarify any issues raised by the care plan presentations.

TERMINAL CARE IN HIV-RELATED ILLNESS

GENERAL OBJECTIVE

On completion of this module the student will be able to address the needs of the person with end-stage HIV infection, who is terminally ill and requires symptom control.

SPECIFIC OBJECTIVES

On completion of this module, the student should be able:

— to demonstrate an understanding of the principles of *palliative* and *terminal care*

— to identify coping strategies for dealing with dying patients, and to understand their use in assisting patients to experience a psychologically acceptable end to their life

— to identify potential personal losses and to apply this awareness to the possible losses experienced by people with HIV infection and AIDS

— to demonstrate an understanding of the role of the nurse in providing palliative and terminal care to people with HIV-related illnesses and their carers.

INTRODUCTION

The number of AIDS cases worldwide has increased to pandemic proportions. The syndrome will affect not only the individuals who are suffering from it, but also the families and friends of these individuals, local communities and health care professionals who are constantly exposed to the death of these people.

As nurses, we are very used to dealing with death from early on in our experience with illness. Death affects individuals in different ways, but HIV poses a unique set of new factors to be faced by patients, carers, families and health professionals.

The aim of this module is to help nurses to examine their feelings about death and losses related to HIV and AIDS, and use this understanding to provide peer group support and to become more effective in providing palliative and terminal care for patients, their relations and friends, and communities affected by AIDS.

LEARNING ACTIVITIES

Learning Activities Key (Module 10)

Learning Activity 1	Principles of Palliative and Terminal Care
Learning Activity 2	Case Studies on Palliative and Terminal Care
Learning Activity 3	The Nurse's Role in Palliative and Terminal Care
Learning Activity 4	Personal Feelings about Life Expectancy Limitations
Learning Activity 5	Personal Experiences of Loss.

Learning Activity 1 PRINCIPLES OF PALLIATIVE AND TERMINAL CARE

BACKGROUND INFORMATION

For people with end-stage HIV infection, there is often nothing that can be done to cure the opportunistic diseases or stop their symptoms. The goal of nursing care, then, is to keep the person as comfortable as possible and relieve as many of the symptoms as possible. This is called palliative care. It is often difficult to decide when aggressive medical treatment should stop and palliative care should begin.

Palliative care might begin, for example:

- when medical treatment is no longer effective or the side-effects outweigh the benefits
- when the person says they do not want to continue aggressive therapy
- when the body's vital organs begin to fail.

The goals of palliative care are:

- to provide the patient with as much control over their symptoms as possible
- to keep the person comfortable and safe
- to assist the person in grieving for and coping with the continuing losses which they are experiencing
- to help the person, their families and carers organize their lives, and orientate them to the forthcoming issues and concerns about dying
- to prepare the person and their loved ones for death.

The nurse must be able to cope with the patient's process of deterioration and dying. This involves being emotionally prepared to accept the inevitable outcome of death. Having others to turn to and an ability to grieve are helpful in dealing with one's own feelings.
It is important for the nurse to change the focus from resolving the underlying pathology and making the person better, to making the process of preparation for the terminal stages as easy and comfortable as possible for all those involved. Palliative care can occur in any setting, including the home.

Terminal care is about caring For the dying patient. Some of the specific interventions and nursing goals are:

COMFORT

- For chronic pain, provide medication in regular doses, not episodically. The drug of choice for chronic pain or for when the patient has difficulty breathing is morphine
- Use relaxation measures such as deep breathing, back rubs, body massages, offering drinks
- Nursing care to keep the person clean and dry
- Position and reposition the person regularly to maintain skin integrity and to prevent formation of contractures..

AUTONOMY

- Accept the person's decisions (such as not eating, refusing or asking for visitors, sitting up or staying in bed)
- Respect their needs for independence by allowing them to do what they can for themselves or in refusing care (such as turning or repositioning).

COPING WITH LOSS AND CHANGE

- Provide support by allowing the person and their family to talk about how they are feeling
- Self-esteem may be enhanced by looking at life achievements and reflecting on positive past events
- Accept people's feelings of anger, grief and other emotions and reactions.

PREPARING FOR DEATH

- If the person asks, and having assessed what they want to know, describe what will happen as he or she nears death. Give reassurance about pain and symptom control, where possible.
- Assist the person and their family in planning details about who needs to be notified aher death and in the organizing of funeral arrangements or a will.

Divide the class into groups of 2 to 4 and ask them to:

- discuss what they understand by
  - a) palliative care
  - b) terminal care
- discuss how they differ.

Then each group should:

- consider nursing interventions which can affect the outcome of:
  a) palliative care
  b) terminal care
- consider the particular needs of patients with end-stage HIV infection in terms of:
  a) palliative care
  b) terminal care
  (groups should look at the holistic needs of patients.)
- consider the facilities, resources, and support groups and care in their communities that can assist them in their provision of care.
- identify medications that are available to provide symptom relief and control, and consider when they can be used.
- consider the social, psychological and spiritual demands, fears and anxieties of patients receiving palliative and terminal care.

What support is available from the community, family and other professionals to deal with these potential problems?

After discussion, reform into a plenary session to compare each group's notes on each point and highlight recurring themes.

Learning Activity 2 CASE STUDIES ON PALLIATIVE AND TERMINAL CARE

Divide the class into 4 smaller groups, and give each group one of the following case studies:

Case Study 1

A male patient under your care has profuse diarrhoea, is nauseated, cannot tolerate any food or drink and is losing considerable weight.
He is married with four children under the age of 8 years. He has lost his job and there are financial concerns. He has strong religious beliefs but has not attended church for many years.

1. What are the needs of this patient?
2. Consider nursing interventions for this patient and family to improve his quality of life.
3. How might you facilitate his care; at home, as an out-patient or as a short-term in-patient?
4. What questions about the future could you ask and how can you, as the nurse, help in his support and care?

Case Study 2

You are caring for a patient in the community who is dying. She is a 20 year-old woman with AIDS, and cannot be offered any further treatment. She is semi-conscious and confined to bed. She lives with her family who feel helpless in caring for her.

1. In what ways can you help this patient to have a comfortable and peaceful death?
2. How can you offer support to her family and reduce their feelings of helplessness?

Learning Activity 3 THE NURSE'S ROLE IN PALLIATIVE AND TERMINAL CARE

Divide the class into small groups and have them discuss the following:

1. Often it seems as if the patient and care-givers want to keep it as secret that the person is going to die, even when it is obvious. Whom are they protecting and do you think this is helpful?
2. Do you feel sufficiently relaxed when talking with patients and families about death and dying? What situations make it easier, and how can you as a nurse facilitate the right environment?
3. Are you able to sit and listen as a person talks about sad or angry feelings, or do you want to say things to make them feel better?
4. What is the role of the nurse in dealing with the body, and with the relatives after death?

The next two learning activities aim to help nurses look at loss and how it might affect them and their lives. Then by relating this to the losses felt by a person with HIV or AIDS, it is hoped that a better understanding will be gained.

Learning Activity 4 PERSONAL FEELINGS ABOUT LIFE EXPECTANCY LIMITATIONS

This is a short exercise which students may choose to do individually or in pairs. Debriefing will be necessary at the end of this activity. Hand the students questionnaires with the following questions:

Questionnaire

1. If you were told you had 10 years to live, what would you like to do in those 10 years?
2. If you were told you had 5 years to live, what would you like to do in those 5 years?

3. If you were told you had six months to live, what would you like to do in those six months?

Consider:

- Are you doing any of these things now? - if not, why not?
- Are you assuming that you will be healthy for these given periods of time?
- How does this questionnaire make you feel?

Get each pair to discuss their findings. Reform the class and discuss the common themes people found. Debrief students and ensure that everyone feels safe prior to completing this Learning Activitv. It is probably better to do this activity in the morning so that the inscructor can check that students are feeling all right by the time they depart at the end of the day.

Learning Activity 5 PERSONAL EXPERIENCES OF LOSS

Before you facilitate this exercise, introduce it to the group as an exercise to help them to understand the losses experienced by people with HIV infection, or by anyone with an experience of chronic or terminal illness.

You will need to allow time for the exercise itself and for the students to talk about the experience. Although it is a group activity, each participant is simulating the loss of very precious parts of their self. The experience can elicit strong feelings of grief, anger and pain. Warn the participants that the exercise is difficult to do and allow individuals to opt out if necessary. Maintain the symbolic nature of the exercise by referring to losses as pieces of paper not as people, roles, etc.

Ask the students to tear a sheet of paper into 16 pieces and write down on each piece one of the following:

— four roles they have which are important to them
— four important people in their lives
— four activities which they find pleasurable
— four material possessions which are important to them.

Ask them to pick one piece of paper from each of the four categories to give up and place them in a box in front of the room.

Have them repeat this "loss" activity, taking another piece of paper from each category.

Now, tell the students that you are going to function as an HIV infection and walk around the room randomly picking up one of the two pieces of paper left in each category from each person.

Divide the class into small groups to share their reactions to the exercises.

Have the students reform the class to discuss their experiences and to explore the issues of loss which the exercise brought up.

As you facilitate the class discussion at the close of this exercise, cover any of the following points if they have not already been made:

1. Dying is only the last of a lifetime of losses which each person must face.
2. The person with HIV infection or AIDS often experiences multiple losses in a very short period of time (ask the students to name same of these).
3. It is important for a person to be able to grieve when he or she experiences loss (the expression of grief may be through anger, bargaining, depression or acceptance).
4. The nurse can give a person an opportunity to grieve, simply by encouraging them to talk, and then listening carefully to them.
5. Nurses experience many losses in their work, particularly in working with people with AIDS.
6. Ask the students to consider how nurses can support each other in grieving for the losses they experience in their work and in their lives as a result of this pandemic. Suggest models such as support groups and discussion groups.

There is a need to debrief after this exercise so that people feel safe before either continuing or finishing.

EDUCATION OF TRADITIONAL PRACTITIONERS TO PREVENT HIV TRANSMISSION THROUGH SKIN-PIERCING PRACTICES

GENERAL OBJECTIVE

On completion of this module, the student should be able to educate traditional practitioners to prevent HIV transmission through skin-piercing procedures.

SPECIFIC OBJECTIVES

On completion of this module, the student should be able:

- to identify practices in a specific community that involve piercing of the skin with reusable instruments
- to identify alternative non-invasive procedures that accomplish the same objective as the above practices
- to identify the cultural and religious values and taboos that prohibit sterilization or instruments or use of alternative practices
- to develop strategies to teach practitioners and the community appropriate procedures to minimize the risks of HIV transmission.

INTRODUCTION

In the same way that invasive procedures performed within the formal health care system may be a route for HIV transmission, the skin-piercing practices performed by traditional practitioners may also cause transmission of the virus.

LEARNING ACTIVITIES

Learning Activities Key (Module 11)

Learning Activity 1 Evaluation of Skin-Piercing Practices
Learning Activity 2 Changing Practices

This module reinforces the role of the nurse in providing community education to prevent HIV transmission.

In *Learning Activity 1*, the students identify risk practices, using criteria established in the instructor's presentation. They then examine cultural values underlying the practice that might impede change and that would need to be taken into consideration when teaching.

In *Learning Activity 2*, the students develop strategies for teaching practitioners and the community the dangers of HIV transmission and the reasons for the use of alternative practices or sterilization procedures.

Learning Activity 1 EVALUATION OF SKIN-PIERCING PRACTICES

Background Information

HIV may be transmitted skin-piercing practices when an instrument is used on more than one person, without proper cleaning or sterilization between uses.

In this situation, small amounts of blood, which may be invisible, could remain on the instrument and be transferred to the next person. It is clear that HIV might be transmitted in exactly the same way as in health care settings by the use of inadequately sterilized needles and syringes.

After presenting the way in which skin-piercing practices can cause the transmission of HIV, ask the class to identify specific examples of such practices. List these on the board.

If the students work in an area in which there are several cultural traditions, list the practices within each specific tradition.

Then, for each practice listed on the board, ask the class:

- to identify who performs the practice
- to describe the cultural importance of the practice in the community
- to determine whether it is possible to make the practice safer in a way that would be acceptable to the practitioner
- to determine alternative acceptable practices.

L-earning Activity 2 DEVELOPING TEACHING STRATEGIES

Changing Practices

The nurse can often play an important role in encouraging changes in the community that benefit peoples health. A lay proctitioner who performs a skin-piercing service may form people without knowing it. The service itself (e.g., traditional methods of treatment, tattooing, infibulation and circumcision) is often believed to be of great value to the people and is on important part of cultural tradition. There maybe reasons for the practice to be performed in a certain way, using material which it would be difficult to pr perly clean and/or sterilize. Traditions are a valuable part of our lives. Nurses need to understand why a practice is done and appreciate its meaning to the people before a safer technique or alternative practice can be suggested.

Changing practices depends on several factors. It depends on the practice, whether it can be done more safely, whether there are alternatives and whether people are likely to give up the practice. Suggesting that people give up a custom must be done very carefully and judiciously since it may jeopardize the nurse's credibility with the community.

Divide the class into two groups. Choose the two most common practices listed on the board, and assign one to each group. Have each group identify a reporter to take notes and report back to the class. Give them 15 minutes to develop strategies for changing the practice. The following questions should be considered:

- How would you approach the practitioner?
- How would you let the person know that you respect him or her?
- How would you present the problem to the practitioner?
- How would you describe the harmful effects of the practice?
- What solutions would you offer?

Have the reporter of group I present its strategies to group 2. Group 2 is to put itself in the place of the practitioner and discuss whether the strategies presented would convince the practitioner or make the practitioner feel upset, and whether it would be possible for the practitioner to implement the proposed strategies. If group 2 has objections to the way in which information is presented or to the information itself, it must explain why and offer an alternative. Encourage constructive criticism and explain that this is an extremely difficult and sensitive topic for which there are no right answers. This will help the students to relax and not be afraid of offering ideas.

The groups should then change roles and duplicate the exercise by presenting the other skin-piercing practice.

An alternative is role-playing. Identify a particular practice and have the class develop strategies for changing the practice. Then have two students role-play a nurse working with a practitioner. After the role-play, ask the practitioner to describe how it felt to hear what the nurse was saying. Then have the observing students offer their positive comments and then their criticisms. Be aware of whether the information is correct, and note the degree of sensitivity with which the message is presented. It is important for the instructor to correct wrong information and to point out messages which are not sensitive.

WHO COUNSELLING GUIDELINES FOR HIV-TESTING

COUNSELLING BEFORE HIV TESTING OR SCREENING

Undergoing a test for HIV infection is likely to be an important step in a person' s life, and should always be accompanied by pre-test and post-test counselling.

The Aim of Pre-test Counselling

Counselling before the test should provide individuals who are considering being tested with information on the technical aspects of screening and the possible personal, medical, social, psychological, and legal implications of being diagnosed as either HIV-positive or HIV-negative. The information should be given in a manner that is easy to understand and should be up to date. Testing should be discussed as a positive act that is linked to changes in risk behaviour.

A decision to be tested should be an informed decision. Informed consent implies awareness of the possible implications of a test result. In some countries, the law requires explicit informed consent before testing can take place; in others, implicit consent is assumed whenever people seek health care. There must be a clear understanding of the policy on consent in every instance, and anyone considering being tested should understand the limits and potential consequences of testing.

Testing for HIV infection should be organized in a way that minimizes the possibility of disclosure of information or of discrimination. In screening, the rights of the individual must also be recognized and respected. Counselling should actively endorse and encourage those rights, both for those being tested and for those with access to the records and results. Confidentiality should be ensured in every instance.

Issues in Pre-test Counselling

Pre-test counselling should focus on two main topics: first, the client's personal history and risk of being or having been exposed to HIV; secondly, assessment of the client's understanding of HIV/AIDS and previous experience in dealing with crisis situations.

Assessment of Risk

In assessing the likelihood that the person has been exposed to HIV, the following aspects of his or her life since about 1980 should be taken into account:

- Frequency and type of sexual behaviour: specific sexual practices, in particular, high risk practices such as vaginal and anal intercourse without use of condoms, unprotected sexual relations with prostitutes;
- Being part of a group with known high prevalence of HIV infection or with known high-risk life-styles, for example, users of injecting drugs, male and female prostitutes and their clients, prisoners, and homosexual and bisexual men;
- Having received a blood transfusion, organ transplant, or blood or body products;
- Having been exposed to possibly non-sterile invasive procedures, such as tattooing and scarification.

Assessment of Psychosocial Factors and Knowledge

The following questions should be asked in assessing the need for HIV testing:

- Why is the test being requested?
- What particular behaviour or symptoms are of concern to the client?
- What does the client know about the test and its uses?
- Has the client considered what to do or how he/she would react if the result is positive, or if it is negative?
- What are the client' s beliefs and knowledge about HIV transmission and its relationship to risk behaviour?
- Who could provide (and is currently providing) emotional social support (family, friends, others)?
- Has the client sought testing before and, if so, when, from whom, for what reason, and with what result?

The initial counselling should include a discussion and assessment of the client's understanding of (a) the meaning and potential consequences of a positive or a negative result, and (b) how a change in behaviour can reduce the likelihood of infection or transmission to others.

Pre-test counselling should include a careful consideration of the person' s ability to cope with the diagnosis and the changes that may need to be made in response to it. It should also encourage the person being counselled to consider why he or she wishes to be tested and what purpose the test will serve. When asking about personal history, it is important to remember that the client:

- may be too anxious to absorb fully what the counsellor says;
- may have unrealistic expectations about the test; and
- may not realize why questions are being asked about private behaviour and therefore be reluctant to answer.

During pre-test counselling, it is also important that the client be told that current testing procedures are not infallible. Both false-positive and false-negative results occur occasionally, although supplementary (confirmatory) tests are very reliable if an initial test is positive. These facts must be clearly explained, together with information about the "window" period during which the test may be unable to assess the true infection status of the person.

IF TESTING IS NOT AVAILABLE

There may be locations where reliable facilities for testing are not readily available . Where this is so, every effort should be made to emphasize prevention counselling, especially the need for changes in behaviour among people who have engaged in high-risk activities, and the reinforcement of appropriate behavioural changes. Counselling, education, information and support are the crux of behaviour change.

COUNSELLING AFTER HIV TESTING OR SCREENING

Counselling after testing will depend on the outcome of the test, which may be a negative result, a positive result, or an equivocal result.

Counselling After A Negative Result

It is very important to discuss carefully the meaning of a negative result (whether this was anticipated or not). The news of being uninfected is likely to produce a feeling of relief or euphoria, but the following points should be emphasized:

Following a possible exposure to HIV, there is a "window" period during which a negative test result cannot be considered reliable. This means that, in most cases, at least three months must have elapsed from the time of possible exposure before a negative test can be considered to mean that infection did not occur. A negative test result carries greatest certainty if at least six months have elapsed since the last possible exposure.

- Further exposure to HIV infection can be prevented only by avoiding high-risk behaviour. Safer sex and avoidance of needle-sharing must be fully explained in a way that is understood and permits appropriate choices to be made.
- Other information on control and avoidance of HIV infection, including the development of positive health behaviour, should be provided. It may be necessary to repeat explanations and for the counsellor and the person being counselled to practise methods of negotiating with others in order to assist the client in introducing and maintaining new behaviour.

Counselling After a Positive Result

People diagnosed as having HIV infection or disease should be told as soon as possible. The first discussion should be private and confidential, and then the client should be given time to absorb the news. After a period of preliminary adjustment, the client should be given a clear, factual explanation of what the news means. This is not a time for speculation about prognosis or estimates of time left to live. It is a time for acknowledging the shock of the diagnosis and for offering and providing support. It is also a time for encouraging hope - hope for achievable solutions to the personal and practical problems that may result . Where resources are available, it may also be justifiable to talk of possible treatments for some symptoms of HIV infection and about the efficacy of anti-viral treatments.

How the news of HIV infection is accepted or incorporated often depends on the following:

1. The person's physical health at the time. People who are ill may have a delayed reaction. Their true response may appear only when they have grown physically stronger.
2. How well the prepared the person was for the news. People who are completely unprepared may react very differently from those who were prepared and perhaps expecting the result. However, even those who are well prepared may experience the reactions described in the following pages.
3. How well supported the person is in the community and how easily he or she can call on friends . Factors such as job satisfaction, family life and cohesion, and opportunities for recreation and sexual contact may all make a difference in the way a person responds. The reaction to the news of HIV

infection may be much worse in people who are socially isolated and have little money, poor work prospects, little family support, and inadequate housing.

4. The person's pre-test personality and psychological condition. Where psychological distress existed before the test result was known, the reactions may be either more or less complicated and require different management strategies than those found in persons without such difficulties. Post-result management should take account of the person's psychological and/or psychiatric history, particularly as the stress of living with HIV may act as a catalyst for the reappearance of earlier disturbance.
   In some cases, news of infection can bring out previously unresolved fears and problems. These can often complicate the process of acceptance and adjustment and will need to be handled sensitively, carefully, and as soon as possible.
5. The cultural and spiritual values attached to AIDS, illness, and death. In some communities with a strong belief in life after death, or with a fatalistic attitude towards life, personal knowledge of HIV infection may be received more calmly than in others. On the other hand, there may be communities in which AIDS is seen as evidence of antisocial or blasphemous behaviour and is thus associated with feelings of guilt and rejection.

Counselling and support are most needed when reactions to the news of HIV infection and disease appear. Some reactions may initially be very intense. It is important to remember that such responses are usually a normal reaction to life-threatening news and as such should be anticipated.

Psychological Issues

The psychological issues faced by most people with HIV infection or disease revolve around uncertainty and adjustment.

With HIV infection, uncertainty emerges with regard to hopes and expectations about life in general, but it may focus on family and job. An even more fundamental uncertainty may concern the quality and length of life, the effect of treatment, and the response of society. All these are relatively unpredictable in terms of their long-term outcome. They need to be discussed openly and frankly, but care should always be taken to encourage hope and a positive outlook.

In response to uncertainty, the person with HIV must make a variety of adjustments. Even the apparent absence of a response may, in itself, be an adjustment through denial. People start to adjust to news of their infection or disease from the time they are first told. Their day-to-day lives will reflect the tension between uncertainty and adjustment. It is this tension that causes other psychosocial issues to assume more or less prominence and intensity from time to time.

- FEAR

People with HIV infection or disease have many fears. The fear of dying and, particularly, of dying alone and in pain is often very evident. Fear may be based on the experiences of loved ones, friends or colleagues who have been ill with, or died of, AIDS. It may also be due to not knowing enough about what is involved and how the problems can be handled. As with most psychological concerns, fear and the pressures such fear creates can often be managed by bringing them clearly and sensitively into the open. They should be discussed in the context of managing the difficulties, including with the help of friends and family or with the counsellor.

- LOSS

People with HIV-related disease experience feelings of loss about their lives and ambitions, their physical attractiveness and potency, sexual relationships, status in the community, financial stability, and independence. As the need for care increases, a sense of loss of privacy and control over life will also be experienced. Perhaps the most common loss that is felt is the loss of confidence. Confidence can be undermined by many aspects of life with HIV, including fear for the future, anxiety about the coping abilities of loved ones and care-givers, by the negative and/or stigmatizing actions of others. For many people, recognition of HIV infection will be the first occasion that forces them to acknowledge their own mortality and physical vulnerability.

- GRIEF

People with HIV infection often have profound feelings of grief about the losses they have experienced or are anticipating. They may also suffer the grief that is projected on to them by close family members, lovers, and friends. Often these same people are supporting and taking care of them on a day-to-day basis, and watching their health decline.

- GUILT

A diagnosis of HIV infection often provokes a feeling of guilt over the possibility of having infected others, or over the behaviour that may have resulted in the infection. There is also guilt about the sadness the illness will cause loved ones and families, especially children. Previous events that may have caused pain or sadness to others and remain unresolved will often be remembered at this time and may cause even greater feelings of guilt.

- DEPRESSION

Depression may arise for a number of reasons. The absence of a cure and the resulting feeling of powerlessness, the loss of personal control that may be associated with frequent medical examinations, and the knowledge that a virus has taken over one's body are all important factors. Similarly, knowing others or about others who have died or are ill with HIV-related disease, and experiencing such things as the loss of potential for procreating and for long-term planning may contribute to depression.

- DENIAL

Some people may respond to news of their infection or disease by denying it. For some people, initial denial can be a constructive way of handling the shock of diagnosis. However, if it persists, denial can become counter-productive, since people may refuse to accept the social responsibilities that go with being HIV-positive.

- ANXIETY

Anxiety can quickly become a fixture in the life of the person with HIV, reflecting the chronic uncertainty associated with the infection. Many of the reasons for anxiety reflect the issues discussed above and concern the following:

— prognosis in the short and long term
— risk of infection with other diseases
— risk of infecting others with HIV
— social, occupational, domestic, and sexual hostility and rejection
— abandonment, isolation, and physical pain
— fear of dying in pain or without dignity
— inability to alter circumstances and consequences of HIV infection
— how to ensure the best possible health in the future
— ability of loved ones and family to cope
— availability of appropriate medical/dental treatment
— loss of privacy and concern over confidentiality
— future social and sexual unacceptability
— declining ability to function efficiently
— loss of physical and financial independence.

- ANGER

Some people become outwardly angry because they feel they have been unlucky to catch the infection. They often feel that they have been, or information about them has been badly or insensitively managed. Anger can sometimes be directed inwardly in the form of self-blame for acquiring HIV, or in the form of self-destructive (suicidal) behaviour.

• SUICIDAL ACTIVITY OR THINKING

People who are HIV-infected have a significantly increased risk of suicide. Suicide may be seen as a way of avoiding pain and discomfort or of lessening the shame and grief of loved ones. Suicide may be active (i .e., deliberate self-injury resulting in death) or passive (i.e., concealing or disregarding the onset of a possibly fatal complication of HIV infection or disease).

• SELF-ESTEEM

Self-esteem is often threatened early in the process of living with HIV. Rejection by colleagues, acquaintances, and loved ones can quickly lead to loss of confidence and social identity, and thus to reduced feelings of self-worth. This can be compounded by the physical impact of HIV-related diseases that cause, for example, facial disfigurement, physical wasting, and loss of strength or bodily control.

• HYPOCHONDRIA AND OBSESSIVE STATES

Preoccupation with health and even the smallest physical changes or sensations can result in hypochondria. This may be transient and limited to the time immediately aher the diagnosis, or it may persist in people who find difficulty in adjusting to the disease.

• SPIRITUAL CONCERNS

Concern about impending death, loneliness, and loss of control may give rise to an interest in spiritual matters and a search for religious support. Expressions of sin, guilt, forgiveness, reconciliation, and acceptance may appear in the context of religious and spiritual discussions.

Many of these and other concerns will appear or become more pronounced when a diagnosis of AIDS is made. The appearance of new infections, cancers, and periods of severe fatigue all have a significant emotional and psychological impact. The effect is likely to be even greater if the person with AIDS has been rejected by family or friends and has withdrawn from normal social relationships.

OTHER COUNSELLING ISSUES

HIV infection often highlights other issues critical to quality of life.

Social Issues

Environmental and social pressures, such as loss of income, discrimination, social stigma (if the diagnosis is becomes commonly known), relationship changes, and changing requirements for sexual expression, may contribute to post-diagnosis psychosocial problems. The patient' s perception of the level and adequacy of social support is of vital concern and may become a source of pressure or frustration.

Medical Management

The type of counselling support usually required and requested is often influenced by the person' s experiences with other forms of health care related to the infection. Where the patient or loved ones feel that medical management has been insensitive or has been conducted without sufficient regard for privacy, counselling may be all the more necessary in order to persuade the patient to comply with recommended treatment programmes.

Counselling may also involve helping the person gain access to appropriate medical care and participate more fully in decisions about treatment. If there is any evidence of neurological disease, day-to-day management of the patient may be complicated, and special emphasis will have to be given to counselling of family, loved ones and care-givers .

At this stage, counsellors may need to co-ordinate a range of health and social services. Many people with HIV will also seek care from traditional or complementary healers: this may first be revealed in the context of supportive counselling. Where this is the case, counselling can help patients talk about their perceived needs and their satisfaction with these care-givers.

Counseling After An Equivocal Test Result

If the result of the HIV test is equivocal, the counsellor has particular responsibilities to provide information. In particular, there are two main issues to cover:

1. The person should be given a clear explanation of what such a test result means. The first test most commonly used on all samples is the enzyme-linked immunosorbent assay (ELISA). The ELISA has levels of sensitivity and specificity approaching 99.5%, meaning that a non-reactive result with this technique can be regarded as a definite indicator that the person is not infected, except for tests during the "window period" . However, a reactive result suggests the possibility of HIV infection . The usual procedure in that case is to perform a second test using the ELISA; if the second ELISA test is also positive, supplementary testing is required, for example using the Western blot test. The results of such supplementary testing may be

positive (indicating HIV infection), negative (indicating no infection), or indeterminate (giving an equivocal result). Where the result of supplementary testing is indeterminate (which may be the case in up to 10% of samples in some areas), the reason may be one of the following:

- the test is cross-reacting with a non-HIV protein (usually, the protein reaction is simulating the reaction associated with p24 care protein).
- there has been insufficient time for full seroconversion to occur since the person was exposed to HIV.

When presented with an indeterminate result, the options are to:

- Use other methods to try to achieve a reliable result. Combinations of laboratory techniques may be needed to exclude false-positive results.
- Refrain from further testing for the moment. If the result is indeterminate and further testing is not possible, the person cannot reliably be considered HIV-infected. The counsellor should advise the person to come for repeat testing in three months. It is important to remember that the risk of finding a false-positive result in the ELISA is higher in areas with a low level of HIV infection than where the background rates of HIV infection are high. Thus, in places where there are many people with AIDS in the community, it is more likely that a reactive or positive result in the ELISA is accurate.

2. Prevention and support while waiting for an unequivocal result. The period of uncertainty following an equivocal test result may be three months or longer. It is important for counsellors to stress essential messages related to prevention of transmission, regarding sexual activity, drug use, donation of body fluids or tissues, and breast-feeding. Just as importantly, however, the uncertainties associated with this period may lead to acute and severe psychosocial difficulties, and the counsellor must be prepared to assess and manage such issues or to make appropriate referrals, if possible.

Self-help Groups

In some places, the counsellor can call on peer-support or self-help groups, part of a growing network of non-governmental AIDS service organizations (ASOs). These can provide a type of personal care and peer-based psychosocial support that may not be available elsewhere. If no such groups exist, the counsellor may be able to encourage clients to form one. Where this is not possible, the counsellor may be able to put clients in touch with each other on an individual basis, at the discretion of the counsellor and with the express consent of the individuals and on a confidential basis. Matters that are often best dealt with through self-help groups, but which need to be raised by the counsellor in any event, include the following:

1. Learning to live with HIV infection. Self-help groups are often in a good position to address this because many of the people involved may have already gone through the process. They can describe the medical and psychological problems they have experienced and the interventions they have found most useful.
2. Helping care-givers and loved ones handle the pressures of living with sick or distressed people on a daily basis, especially where this involves managing bleeding, vomiting, incontinence, disposal of dressings, etc., and advice regarding sexual relations.
3. Reducing stress and avoiding conflict. The need to overcome anxiety, depression and other possible challenges to sustained health has to be handled on a practical, "I did this..." basis.
4. Deciding how best to talk about HIV/AIDS. Fears of disclosing a diagnosis of HIV or AIDS to loved ones, family, friends, and colleagues need to be examined and solutions sought, including what to say, to whom, when, and how.
5. Dealing with feelings of loneliness, depression, and powerlessness. Self-help or peer–support groups can provide help and mutual support. Advice from people who have themselves gone through such feelings may be more meaningful than advice provided on a second-hand or theoretical basis.
6. Managing the implications of adopting and maintaining safer sex behaviour. Peer-support groups can organize discussions and training that can be far more relevant than advice provided through formal health care programmes. Peer commitment to safer sex also helps make these practices socially acceptable, attractive and thus sustainable.

The essence of peer-support group activity is a feeling of group cohesion, a sharing of experiences and mutually supportive activities. At times, such groups may need help in getting started and in maintaining regular activities. They will all look to the counsellor for help in identifying medical services and care-givers. Providing legal advice and, in some cases, financial support may also become issues in establishing such groups and giving them operational legitimacy.

CONSENSUS STATEMENT FROM THE WHO/ UNICEF CONSULTATION ON HIV TRANSMISSION AND BREAST-FEEDING

In view of the importance of breast milk and breast-feeding for the health of infants and young children, the increasing prevalence of human immunodeficiency virus (HIV) infection around the world, and recent data concerning HIV transmission through breast milk, a Consultation on HIV Transmission and Breast-feeding was held by WHO and UNICEF from 30 April to 1 May 1992. Its purpose was to review currently available information on the risk of HIV transmission through breast milk and to make recommendations on breast-feeding.

Based on the various studies conducted to date, roughly one-third of the babies born worldwide to HIV-infected women become infected themselves, with this rate varying widely in different populations. Much of this mother-to-infant transmission occurs during pregnancy and delivery, and recent data confirm that some occurs through breast-feeding. However, the large majority of babies breast-fed by HIV-infected mothers do not become infected through breast milk. Recent evidence suggests that the risk of HIV transmission through breast-feeding (a) is substantial among women who become infected during the breast-feeding period, and (b) is lower among women already infected at the time of delivery. However, further research is needed to quantify the risk of HIV transmission through breast-feeding and determine the associated risk factors in both of these circumstances.

Studies continue to show that breast-feeding saves lives. It provides impressive nutritional, immunological, psychosocial and child-spacing benefits. Breast-feeding helps protect children from dying of diarrhoeal diseases, pneumonia and other infections. For example, artificial or inappropriate feeding is a major contributing factor in the 1.5 million annual infant deaths from diarrhoeal diseases. Moreover, breast-feeding can prolong the interval between births and thus make a further contribution to child survival, as well as enhancing maternal health.

It is, therefore, important that the baby' s risk of HIV infection through breast-feeding be weighed against its risk of dying of other causes if it is denied breast-feeding. In each country, specific guidelines should be developed to facilitate the assessment of the circumstances of the individual woman.

Recommendations

1. In all populations, irrespective of HIV infection rates, breast-feeding should continue to be protected, promoted and supported.
2. Where the primary causes of infant deaths are infectious diseases and malnutrition, infants who are not breast-fed run a particularly high risk of dying from these conditions. In these settings, breast-feeding should remain the standard advice to pregnant women, including those who are known to be HIV-infected, because their baby ' s risk of becoming infected through breast milk is likely to be lower than its risk of dying of other causes if deprived of breast-feeding. The higher a baby's risk of dying during infancy, the more protective breast-feeding is and the more important it is that the mother be advised to breast-feed. Women living in these settings whose particular circumstances would make alternative feeding an appropriate option might wish to know their HIV status to help guide their decision about breast-feeding. In such cases, voluntary and confidential HIV testing accompanied in all cases by pre- and post-test counselling could be made available where feasible and affordable.
3. In settings where infectious diseases are not the primary causes of death during infancy, pregnant women known to be infected with HIV should be advised not to breast-feed but to use a safe feeding alternative for their babies. Women whose infection status is unknown should be advised to breast-feed. In these settings, where feasible and affordable, voluntary and confidential HIV testing should be made available to women along with pre- and poste-test counselling, and they should be advised to seek such testing before delivery.
4. When a baby is to be artificially fed, the choice of substitute feeding method and product should not be influenced by commercial pressures. Companies are called on to respect this

principle in keeping with the International Code of Marketing of Breast milk Substitutes and all relevant World Health Assembly resolutions. It is essential that all countries give effect to the principles and aim of the International Code. If donor milk is to be used, it must first be pasteurized and, where possible, donors should be tested for HIV. When wet-nursing is the chosen alternative, care should be taken to select a wet-nurse who is at low risk of HIV infection and, where possible, known to be HIV-negative.

5. HIV-infected women and men have broad concerns, including maintaining their own health and well-being, managing their economic affairs, and making future provision for their children, and, therefore, require counselling and guidance on a number of important issues. Specific issues to be covered by counselling include infant feeding practices, the risk of HIV transmission to the offspring if the woman becomes pregnant, and the transmission risk from or to others through sexual intercourse or blood. All HIV-infected adults who wish to avoid childbearing should have ready access to family planning information and services.
6. In all countries, the first and overriding priority in preventing HIV transmission from mother to infant is to prevent women of childbearing age from becoming infected with HIV in the first place. Priority activities are (a) educating both women and men about how to avoid HIV infection for their own sake and that of their future children; (b) ensuring their ready access to condoms; (c) providing prevention and appropriate care for sexually transmitted diseases, which increase the risk of HIV transmission; and (d) otherwise supporting women in their efforts to remain uninfected.

•••